Manipulation

*How to Master the Art of Analyzing People
and Influence Human Behavior with
Dark Psychology and Mind Control Techniques*

Table of Contents

Introduction:
Leveling the Playing Field with Psychology's Darkest Secrets

You are being manipulated.

This is a fact.

Every day, every hour, in countless ways, you are being manipulated.

Politicians work to manipulate you into supporting them. Companies try and manipulate you into giving them your hard-earned money. Employers do all they can to convince you to do more hard work for less money. Romantic partners manipulate you into doing what they want to do instead of what you want to do.

Manipulation takes on many forms. It comes with different degrees of risk and levels of severity. The differences can be so vast that it might feel positively criminal to call them by the same term. But it's important to show intellectual clarity by recognizing that all attempts to control someone can rightly be called manipulation.

Is my use of the word "manipulation" unnerving you? The word does have a negative connotation. Only bad people manipulate.

Dictators manipulate the populace into action, while heroic leaders convince knowledgeable voters to follow the better angels of their nature.

Right?

Or could it be that this sort of linguistic hair-splitting is just another example of how manipulation works? Words are massaged carefully by manipulators so that they can wiggle their way out of sticky situations.

One person's manipulation is another's persuasion. But as Shakespeare once wrote, "A rose by any other name would smell as sweet."

In this book we will be looking at manipulation as a brute fact of life.

Manipulation is a tool. I would argue that like any other tool, manipulation in and of itself is neither good nor bad. A hammer can be used to build a cradle or a coffin. A gun can be used to fend off robbers or to commit robbery.

Some of you may be worried that this book will be used by disreputable people to commit nefarious deeds. So let me take a moment and handle these concerns by addressing any rogues that might have this book in their hands.

This book is not to be used to harm anyone. The powerful information within these pages could be very dangerous if it fell into the wrong hands, so check to make sure your hands are clean before reading onward. If you have any negative inclinations whatsoever, then I would ask you to put down the book and seek professional help immediately.

Thank you for your cooperation.

Alright, are all the bad people gone?

Please understand that I know what you're probably thinking right now. You think I sound foolish. The sort of bad people who manipulate others in evil ways aren't going to listen to my pleas. They're just going to press onward, doing whatever they want to do no matter what I might say about the matter.

And that's exactly the point.

All of the information in this book is already available to anyone with the eyes to see. People were practicing the art of manipulation long before the first writing system was ever devised.

Sociopaths with a lust for power and a lack of concern for morality don't need books like this. They can learn to manipulate people the old fashioned way, by toying with those around them.

The people who will benefit most from this book are those that are hesitant to even think of manipulating another soul. They've listened to the teachers who say that manipulation is evil and that even researching the topic might harm your soul in some way. Oddly enough, such leaders often find it hard to explain why their threats and appeals to authority don't qualify as manipulation.

Manipulation deals with the cold hard facts of human nature, and hiding such facts doesn't protect anyone. It actually makes people more vulnerable. Who is easier to rob, someone who has been taught about the ways of robbers or someone who has been taught to pretend as if such people don't even exist?

This book will teach you about the way the human mind works and how it can be manipulated. What you do with this information is up to you. In a perfect world, only pure souls would be left after my heartfelt plea earlier in this introduction.

But we don't live in a perfect world. We live in the real world. A world that is flooded with manipulation. And we're not talking about just any flood, we're talking about a flash flood that is violent, unpredictable, and relentless. If you want to keep your head above water, then you need to catch up fast.

Chapter 1:
Understanding Dark Psychology

"People will do anything, no matter how absurd, in order to avoid facing their own souls. One does not become enlightened by imagining figures of light, but by making the darkness conscious."

— Carl Jung, Psychology and Alchemy

The human mind is one of the most complex objects known to mankind. It is something we all know intimately, and yet few people truly understand how it works. Even in this age of high science we still have a frighteningly limited understanding of just what goes on inside the human mind.

Still, the fact that many things are unknown doesn't mean that the mind is unknowable.

Psychology has developed to show us how the mind works. Go to any bookstore and you'll find countless tomes helping to explain the natural thought patterns that develop within each of us and propel us down the many roads of our lives.

But while there are many things you can learn from psychology textbooks, there are also things that you will not learn.

In psychology's shadow, a sister science has been growing. While psychology is focused on explaining how the mind works, dark psychology has developed to explain how the mind might be manipulated.

Imagine that the mind is a computer game. Most psychological texts are like the guides and rule books that are written to tell people how to play the game within "acceptable" parameters. They might help you beat the game, but they are still encouraging you to beat the game by playing by the rules.

Dark psychology is more like a book of cheats. Instead of showing you how to play along with the game, dark psychology shows you how to find loopholes, hacks, and ways to rewrite the rules.

This is the power of dark psychology and the reason why it is feared and suppressed. The world is set up to encourage people to play by the rules, even though the individuals who see the greatest success are those that break the rules and thereby rewrite them. Many of the people with power over you gained that power using dark psychology, and they are afraid that if you gain access to the same tools they will lose their advantage.

If you are like most people, you have lived your life according to the rules. But have you ever thought about the sort of people who wrote the rules in the first place? How many governments have been founded by revolutionaries who seized power and went to work setting up a system to suppress future revolutionaries?

Is Dark Psychology a Real Thing?

If you have never heard the words "dark psychology," then you might be skeptical that such a thing even exists. It sounds so fantastic, like something out of a Hollywood movie. But as any scientist will tell you, the truth is more fantastic than anything a

Tinseltown screenwriter could devise. Dark psychology is all too real, and if you choose to ignore it then you do so at your own risk.

This isn't to say that everyone agrees about what dark psychology is. The fact of the matter is that dark psychology is a controversial subject. Open up your average psychology 101 textbook and you're probably not going to find these two words used.

One reason that dark psychology isn't a widespread topic is because of the danger surrounding the matter. We are discussing tools that have been used by some of the most dangerous individuals in human history. Many psychological professionals are willing to look at what might drive an individual to turn to manipulation, but few want to map out just how that manipulation takes place. This might come from an understandable fear, but letting fear control your actions can also lead to dangerous places. Those who use dark psychology count on having fearful marks that they can prey upon. If you want to move beyond the reach of such individuals, then you need to be willing to go places that others won't.

This book was written from a place of such willingness. You'll find honest truths in this book that you won't find in others. The facts are all out there, but they are often disconnected, sugar-coated, or spun in such a way that the reality behind them becomes unclear.

If you are worried about whether or not you can trust this book, then you're already starting to learn its lesson. Every human being comes to the table with their own biases. The scientific method can help to counteract human failings and home in on objective truths, but even that powerful tool can fall short. A short look into the ongoing "reproducibility crisis" shows that many of the social science facts that we are taught aren't as well attested as you might believe (Yong, 2018).

The best way to see whether or not dark psychology is true is to learn about the basic ideas and ask yourself whether or not they map onto reality as you know it. Once you learn about the fundamental principles, you'll be able to look at the world around you and understand it in greater depth.

Let's begin with one of the fundamental facts of dark psychology: you do not have complete control.

We are taught from a young age that our choices are all our own, but if you learn about modern neurological models you'll quickly see that things are more complicated. We aren't little gods making choices in a void. We are all the products of our genetics, our environment, and our past choices.

This might seem like the cold and materialistic view, but you can see shades of this thinking throughout the entirety of mankind's intellectual history. The Apostle Paul in Romans 7:15 was recorded as saying, "I do not understand what I do. For what I want to do I do not do, but what I hate I do."

While this verse has been seen from many angles over the centuries, one particularly keen observation that anyone, religious or not, can recognize is the understanding that every human is conflicted.

Those who practice dark psychology understand this fact. They recognize that humans can be made to do things that they despise if the situation is right.

Think to your own life. Have you ever hurt people you loved? Have you known what you needed to do and then done something completely different? Do these seem like the actions of a logical being?

The simple answer is that humans aren't logical beings. We are a bundle of contradictory needs and wants. Our higher thinking sits on top of instincts and desires that evolved in the jungles and plains of Africa. We may have put on clothes and put up walls to separate ourselves from the other animals, but we haven't been able to wall off the animistic areas of our own minds.

While the exact origins of life on Earth and human consciousness are both highly contentious areas of debate, the basic story I have told you is indisputable. Whether you believe that human beings are made of matter alone or some combination of matter and spirit, thinkers of all stripes have come to understand that the human mind can be manipulated. While our most celebrated thinkers are those that have sought ways to elevate our minds and move beyond our baser instincts, the most successful leaders tend to be those that know how to speak to every level of human existence.

The ability to tap into the deepest levels of human consciousness can be defined as dark psychology. It deals with the areas of the mind that we treat like the closets, basements, and attics of our mental homes. They are the areas we ignore. And because we ignore them, they are great places for intruders to sneak in and take up residence.

One of the things you should do while reading this book is take time to try and delve into the darker recesses of your mind. Put aside distractions and value judgments and try and see how your mind works. The world is so busy these days that many people don't have anything close to a real understanding of how thoughts arise within their own mind.

Time spent in open silence with your own mind will reveal a world of thoughts that you normally suppress or ignore during normal life. With enough digging you will be able to excavate layers of thoughts and emotions that normally go completely unaddressed in the grind of daily living. These are parts of yourself that you can try to ignore but can't erase.

They are the parts of your mind that manipulators will target.

Once you realize how little people know of their own minds, it becomes easy to understand why the topic of dark psychology is so secretive. Most people don't want to deal with the darkness and complexity inside of them. And that means that those who are willing to get down and dirty can end up wielding a tremendous amount of power.

Why Dark Psychology Matters

The most important thing to understand about dark psychology is that its principles are in effect whether you believe in them or not. Think of gravity. Even if you were to spend the rest of your life announcing to the world that you don't believe in gravity and avoiding any scientific discussion on the matter, if you went out and tried to jump off of a building you'd still fall to the ground like anyone else. While different scientists can debate the terminology used to refer to dark psychology, the most basic concepts are indisputable facts. And facts don't care about feelings.

The other factor to consider is that many of the people who control your life understand dark psychology. They might have learned about it through a book like this or they could have naturally developed a personality that can use dark psychology with the ease that most of us use language. Such individuals exist, as frightening as the idea might be.

Every day you are competing for success with individuals who are willing to use dark psychology to their own advantage. Whenever you log onto the internet, turn on your television, or look out your window, you are likely to be flooded with ideas and imagery rooted in dark psychology. Both the people who are currently in control of your country and those that seek to control your country are utilizing dark psychology to achieve their goals.

While only a small percentage of the population have the sort of extreme psychological disorders that lead to the most destructive forms of dark psychology, the fact is that some of the most extreme personalities can lead to power and success. It takes a unique type of person to climb the deadly ladders of modern politics and business. Even if just 1% of the population naturally utilizes dark psychology, modern society is set up so that 1% of the population can control the other 99%.

One of the reasons that dark psychology can be difficult to recognize is because of how widespread it is. There's also the fact that we are engulfed in our day to day psychological battles, to the point where dark psychology can be difficult to recognize.

Do you think most fish know anything about the scientific properties of water? Since they spend their lives surrounded by it, they learn to work with it without ever needing to learn the underlying nature of the material.

The same goes for humans and psychology. We spend our whole lives dealing with the nature of our own minds and the minds of those around us. This allows us to develop a certain natural aptitude, but it can keep us from seeing the big picture.

Learning about dark psychology is all about stepping out of the water and looking down into it with clear and unclouded eyes. It's about stripping away the biases that you have developed both consciously and unconsciously throughout your life. It's about learning to see things as they really are and not how you or anyone else would like them to be.

A Way of Empowering Yourself

How can you avoid dangers that you can't see?

Would you put on a blindfold before stepping into a cage full of crocodiles? Of course not! But that's exactly what people are doing when they go through life ignorant of matters such as dark psychology. They are like children who think that if they can't see you then you can't see them.

You are surrounded by manipulators who are constantly using the tools of dark psychology to change the way you behave. This might be hard to believe, but once you learn about how dark psychology works, you'll start to see it everywhere.

In addition to using your new knowledge defensively, you can also take what you learn and go on the offensive. Think of a political figure from history that you admire. Even though I don't know who you have in mind, I can say with absolute confidence that they used dark psychology.

Let's look at one clear example of a beloved figure, Abraham Lincoln. Here is a man so beloved and respected that he became known as "honest Abe." And yet during the fight to pass the amendment to abolish slavery, he lied to congress. They asked him if ambassadors from the South were on their way to discuss a peace treaty and he said that "So far as I know, there are no peace commissioners in the city, or likely to be in it" (Vorenberg, 2004, pp. 205-206).

Notice the careful use of language. It's a masterful lawyerly sort of lie, true on a technical level but clearly violating the spirit of the question asked. Whether the statement was true or not it gave the members of congress a false idea of reality. And I would bet most people would say that deliberately warping someone's perception of reality to get them to behave as you'd like them to qualifies as manipulation.

But who today would be upset that Abraham Lincoln manipulated a group of pro-slavery politicians in order to free millions of innocent men, women, and children?

The term dark psychology has negative connotations, but that's mainly because the most noticeable examples of it are those that are evil and destructive. When we don't like what someone is doing, then it's easy to call out their manipulations, but if we agree with them then we prefer to imagine they are beyond such base behavior.

If you want true understanding and the power that comes with it, you must first put away your preconceptions. Don't be in such a hurry to label things as right and wrong. This doesn't mean that you have to throw out your sense of morality, it simply means that you should take the time to see the world as it truly is before you start fretting about how it should be.

The easiest way to think about the world is in terms of black and white, but any careful examination of the realities we face on a daily basis reveals that there are many shades of gray that complicate our every moral calculation. If we lived in a fairy tale world of only good and evil, then maybe matters such as dark psychology would be better off ignored. But we don't live in that kind of world, with every moral answer available to us. We often face situations where we feel the need to choose between the lesser of two evils.

If you have a full understanding of dark psychology, then you may find that new choices open up to you. Those that can persuade others don't need to stick with the options directly in front of them, they can cut through arbitrary limitations and find a third way.

Before moving on, there is one last concern that we should address. Some of you might be afraid that if you learn about dark psychology it may corrupt you in some way. You might believe that if you learn how dark manipulators work you may become a dark manipulator yourself.

Once again, while studying this topic, you should take the time to look within yourself. Ask yourself whether or not you are someone who secretly wants to hurt other people. If hateful thoughts arise don't immediately suppress them, just try and observe them as they are.

If you find that you do have dark thoughts and impulses inside of you, then you should be wary about how you move forward. But you should also understand that just ignoring reality will not change a thing. Pretending that your dark side doesn't exist won't erase it from being, just as ignoring dark psychology won't magically erase it from existence.

You may find that learning about the dark side of humanity in general and yourself in particular will actually help you to keep the dark side in check. This is something many students of martial arts learn. You would think that people who learn how to fight would feel the need to go out and flex their muscles by getting into fights. But many students have actually discovered that a proper understanding of martial arts helps to alleviate the need to prove themselves in a fight.

Once you understand humanity on a deeper level, then you can act from a position of clarity rather than ignorance. You will understand that many people behave badly because they don't know better, whether they are slaves to their own base instincts or the manipulations of others. Once you see these people as they are, you will pity them rather than hating them.

Any hunter knows that an animal is at its most dangerous when it is fearful, and fear is commonly caused by ignorance. With knowledge, you can banish destructive fears from your mind. With persuasion, you can learn to create peaceful solutions to potentially dangerous conflicts. When good people understand the rules of dark psychology, the world can become a better place.

Still, you shouldn't take anything for granted. You should always be on guard against threats from both inside and out. This book can teach you about how dark psychology works, but it can't give you the character needed to wield this knowledge in a constructive and not destructive manner.

In closing, knowledge is power. Learning about dark psychology is highly empowering. What you do with that power is up to you.

Chapter 2:
Mind Control

"For, after all, how do we know that two and two make four? Or that the force of gravity works? Or that the past is unchangeable? If both the past and the external world exist only in the mind, and if the mind itself is controllable – what then?"

— George Orwell

The phrase "mind control" conjures images out of science fiction films. You might picture aliens shooting out rays of light to create a horde of minions. Or maybe you imagine a doctor tying a person down and forcing them to stare at flashing images on a screen that will reprogram their way of thinking.

The truth is more frightening than fiction.

Real life mind control is much more subtle than fictional mind control. No one needs to shoot lasers at you, they just need to speak words. The method of control seeps in through your ears and goes to work on your mind, sight unseen.

The good news is that you don't need any gadgets or gizmos to beat mind control efforts. The first step to protecting yourself is learning about the weapons arrayed against you.

Detected Versus Undetected Mind Control

To understand mind control, it helps to divide it into two categories: detected versus undetected. Detected mind control refers to any attempt made to control another person's mind that is either up-front and honest or obvious.

The most obvious example of a case of detected mind control is the sort of act you'll see when you go to a hypnotist for therapeutic or entertainment purposes. The hypnotist will announce that they are going to take control of your mind and then they will do just that. People who would be totally afraid of making a fool of themselves in a public speaking scenario will cluck like chickens for the amusement of peers and complete strangers.

Just about everyone has seen a hypnotist at worked, clapped in approval, and then gone about their day. But have you ever taken a moment to think about the implications of this sort of act?

Here we have individuals who have trained themselves in the art of mind control. They have gotten good enough that they can go up to strangers and convince them to do things they would never have done of their own accord. And hypnotists are practicing the most blatant sort of detected mind control! Imagine what dark psychology practitioners can achieve using undetected mind control.

Other forms of detected mind control include commercials, sales pitches, and debates. These are situations where you are dealing with a person or group that is clearly trying to get you to take some action or change your mind. People often dislike these situations because they don't like the idea of someone trying to bend them to their will, but the fact is that these scenarios are some of the most honest we encounter in our lives. True, the people involved want something from you, but they are relatively upfront about their desires and so you can guard yourself as needed.

The truth is that the most dangerous scenarios are those where the other party seems to have no ulterior motive. In these situations you can find it easy to let your guard down, and once you do a skilled manipulator will make their move.

Undetected Mind Control

Doing mind control out in the open might be a more ethical way to try and get people to change their minds and behavior, but most manipulators will tell you that they aren't concerned with ethics. This is why they would prefer that their efforts went undetected.

The basic idea is that if you think you are dealing with someone who is trying to change your mind, you will have your mental guard up. The human mind reacts to challenging ideas in a way that is similar to facing down dangerous attackers. But if you don't recognize a threat, then you won't put in the effort needed to be skeptical and defensive about what is coming your way.

So the job of a manipulator is to find a way to mask their real intentions. For a creative individual with an understanding of dark psychology, the possibilities are nearly endless.

One way to hide manipulation efforts is by putting on the right costume. In the most open cases of mind control, the "teams" that exist are clear to anyone who can see. In traditional marketing it's easy to tell the salesman from the potential customers. But undetected mind control will usually muddy the waters, blurring the distinction between the different "teams" until people don't know who to trust.

Consider the modern marketing environment. If you are looking to make a purchase today, you need to be careful when searching for product reviews. You can never really be sure whether or not you are reading a review that has been written by an honest consumer, or if you're reading a piece of marketing that has been planted by the product's creator or their competition. Companies hire reviewers every day to write glowing reviews for their own goods and services or harsh reviews for their competitors.

This is just one clear and understandable attempt at mind control. They can get much more subtle and nefarious.

Another approach that a manipulator might take is by trying to convince the target that their idea is actually the target's own. They will start by getting a sense of what the target believes, mirroring each belief along the way until the target believes that they are on the same page as the manipulator. Once the manipulator has gained the target's trust, they will then subtly steer the conversation toward the manipulator's goal. This sort of approach may sound like it should be obvious, but the skilled manipulator knows how to be subtle and subversive. The conversation shifts by subtle degrees until the target begins to believe that they themselves have come up with the idea that the manipulator has been pushing for all along.

The one thing that ties just about every piece of undetected mind control together is dishonesty. Even if the manipulators aren't technically lying, they are still withholding the full story. The manipulator thrives in areas where people believe they can trust what they are hearing. If trust can be established, then the manipulator has practically won already. This is why it's important that you be slow to trust. One of the best tools you can use in the fight against dark psychology is a healthy level of skepticism.

Lifting The Curtain

The good news is that there isn't a permanent wall between these two categories. There might be undetected mind control efforts going on all around you, but that doesn't mean that they must always remain undetected.

By developing your understanding of dark psychology and your powers of perception, you can start to detect the mind control efforts that are going on all around you. Things that are hidden can be revealed if you have the eyes to see.

One final thing to keep in mind is that the line between calculated manipulation and normal human behavior can be thin. Everyone has goals and desires and will work to get what they want.

The sad truth is that there is no easy way to tell whether or not someone is a manipulator. Detecting malicious individuals is a talent that must be developed through years of practice and study. You must constantly observe people, watching what they do and how they do it. While you can learn a lot about someone in a relatively short period of time, you may still have to watch them for days, weeks, or even months before you can decide whether or not they are living honest lives or working to manipulate those around them for their own purposes.

The only way to learn how to quickly and accurately identify signs of dark manipulation is by putting in the work and learning with each passing day.

Media: Mind Control Masters

The media game is the manipulation game. Mass media only exists because it has the power to control the narrative and convince people to take certain actions. Would giant companies spend millions of dollars on advertising if they didn't have a good reason to believe that those ads would convince people to pay for their products?

Artists have always used their talents to control the passions of their fellow citizens, but today the power of mass media has taken things to an entirely new level. The television set has become a mind control device that people will willingly subject themselves to.

How did we get here?

The Danger of Poetics

To understand the current media landscape, it helps to turn back the clock to a simpler time. Around 2400 years ago, the Greek philosopher Plato wrote *The Republic*, a book in which he tried to imagine an ideal society. One of the many controversial arguments in the book was that poets had no place in the perfect state. He recognized the beauty of poetry, but argued that this was what made it so dangerous. A poet could dress up a lie, make it look beautiful, and convince people to go along with it.

You may not feel like the actors, anchors, pundits, and pontificators that you see on television are worthy of the title of poet, but they still serve the role that Plato described in his ancient classic. The members of the media have carefully honed their talents of manipulation over hundreds of years. From yellow journalism, to reality TV, and click bait, every generation of media artists has pushed the envelope of just how the public could be cajoled into falling in line with their manufactured narratives.

Stepping Back From The Screen

This isn't to say that everyone on TV is evil. Once again, we must put morality aside so that we can recognize manipulation even when it is being used to achieve goals that we agree with. To argue that it's not really manipulation because the ends justify the means is to purposefully cloud your own vision. Do you want to see the world as it is or as you'd like it to be?

Carefully observing the media is one of the best ways to learn the art of dark manipulation. Just be careful, because even if you know the tricks that are being used you can still get swept up by them. If you want to maintain your mental freedom, then you must be constantly vigilant.

If you want to protect yourself from mind control, then one of the best things you can do is to limit your media diet. Social media, 24/7 news channels, and all outrage-based reporting are especially dangerous. Try and find outlets that seek to tell you what is happening rather than telling you how to feel about things. While every media source has their own biases, the less emotionally charged things are the larger the role your critical mind can play in your media diet.

Common Techniques

If you want to defend yourself against mind control, the first thing you need to do is understand the tools manipulators use to gain command over unwitting minds. While some of these techniques can still be powerful even when they are recognized, the simple understanding of what is being done can help you avoid them or minimize their damage.

Social Separation

Human beings are social creatures by nature. We evolved in groups of dozens of individuals. This explains why most humans require regular social contact with a varied group of individuals to live healthy and fulfilled lives. It's also why manipulators will work to consciously sever ties between the person they're targeting and that individual's social safety net.

Mind control is all about establishing authority. This is difficult to do when there is competition for the position. If someone hears something from a manipulator and then goes to their parents, friends, and other respected individuals for additional input, then there's a good chance that one of those people will contradict the manipulator's message. Even if the manipulator has built up a position of high value and esteem, any dissenting voice can put some doubt into the mind of the manipulated and threaten the entire scheme.

Manipulators understand the power of social pressure, which is why they do what they can to remove normal social pressure and replace it with something that they control. This is why cult leaders will encourage members to break off contact with the outside world and dive deeper into the controlled environment of the cult. It's the reason why political prisoners are often placed into solitary confinement, so that they can't discuss what is happening with any of their fellow dissenters. It is the reason why abusers will force the person they're abusing to choose between them and their family. An isolated individual is a weakened individual, and weakened individuals are easy prey for talented manipulators.

If anyone ever asks you to choose between them and your family, watch out. The moment you separate yourself from your family and friends, you become much more susceptible to mind control in all of its forms. Maintaining a healthy social support system is one of the best ways to defend against manipulation.

Emotional Extremes

The opposite of love isn't hate, it's apathy.

There is a reason why many romance stories depict the two main characters in conflict at some point. Love and hate may seem to be as far apart as you can get on the emotional spectrum, but the truth is that both emotions are closer than you might think. They are both strong, powerful emotions that can lead to obsession.

Manipulators understand that if they want to get their hooks into someone's mind, they can't use tepid emotions. They will engage the individual by using emotional extremes. This will be further heightened by the strategy of swinging between emotions rapidly to create a sense of contrast that makes every emotion all that much more forceful.

This is commonly seen in the "hot and cold" approach used by manipulators. At first the manipulator will be highly positive with their target, showering them with effusive praise and affection. Once the target has become acclimated to this positive approach and comes to expect it, the manipulator will switch up their approach, withdrawing all positive reinforcement. This leaves the target feeling lost, suddenly cut off from the positive emotions they have come to expect.

While most people experience natural mood swings from time to time, a manipulator will change their mood strategically. If you notice that someone around you seems to switch between emotional extremes, you should definitely ask yourself why this might be happening. It could be a natural part of their psychology, or they could be using their emotions to dig deep into your mind. Pay special attention for individuals who turn negative when they aren't getting what they want and only act positively once you have given them what they want.

Rhythm and Repetition

Life has a rhythm all its own. Think of the beating of your heart, the steady pattern of your footsteps, and the rhythmic pattern of the seasons. One of the reasons we love music so much is because patterns speak to us on a deep level. It's also the reason why most religious ceremonies include songs, chants, and other rhythmic patterns.

Today the patterns developed by artists and priests have been recognized by modern science. Many therapists, psychologists, and other psychological professionals use "verbal repetition" to induce hypnotic states ("Hypnosis", 2018). Once you're in such a state, you are more open to suggestion. This means you're more open to doing and believing things that you might not have been open to beforehand. This is why people often use repetition when meditating on things they would like to do and achieve. But while hypnosis can be used constructively, it can also be used destructively.

Practitioners of dark psychology can use hypnotic repetition to lull people into a false sense of security. Once their mental guards are down, the manipulator will start telling them what to believe, what they should do, and even how they should feel. If the right mood has been created, then incredible shifts of consciousness can be achieved, which further elevates the manipulator in the mind of the manipulated.

This technique is especially powerful because even consciously skeptical individuals can fall prey to it. The tools of music can be put to use to leapfrog over the conscious mind and get at the subconscious of an individual. If you start hearing drums, chanting, or even particularly rhythmic speech patterns, then it might be best to cover your ears and walk away. You never know what might happen if the music takes control.

Physical Attacks

While mental attacks are the most common tool of the manipulator's trade, this doesn't mean that they are beyond using physical violence. The use of physical pain is one of the oldest tricks in the manipulation game.

The human body is programmed to avoid pain at all costs. It's this drive that helps us stay alive, avoiding potentially deadly threats. This fact can be used by manipulators to help reshape the thinking of their targets. Physical pain can be used to wear down individuals to the point where they are more open to the suggestions of the person doing the manipulation.

It's important to understand that physical pain can be subtle. While there are plenty of extreme cases where manipulators turn into torturers to achieve their goals, there are even more cases where violence is used in more limited and strategic ways.

While all the tools of mind control can be dangerous, physical violence is widely considered to be one of the worst. This is especially true when the manipulator is near and dear to the person being manipulated. No one should ever physically abuse another person, no matter how subtle the violence might seem. If you are in a relationship and you notice that things seem to be turning violent, then you should immediately attempt to remove yourself from contact and seek professional help. Your life, your health, and your sanity are too valuable to risk.

Subconscious Manipulation

While you should definitely watch out for direct attacks on your mental integrity, you should also stay on your guard for any sign of subconscious or subliminal manipulation. Skilled manipulators will slip subtle messages into interactions that you might not notice on a conscious level, but you must know that your subconscious will pick up what is being laid out.

While we are used to dealing with direct and obvious messages in the form of written or spoken words, a lot can be conveyed using other methods. Visual artwork is as popular as it is because just one glance at a striking image can convey a message that no speech could ever fully get across. The same goes for a powerful pose, a subtle shift in expression, or a costume change that happens to change the entire mood. The skilled manipulator knows how to use every tool available to them to get their point across.

Imagery is another thing to watch out for. A painting in the background or a picture that flashes by for just an instant in an advertisement, these sort of techniques can imprint on your subconscious without alerting your active mind. You don't know exactly what happened, but if you pay close attention, you can feel the shift happen within yourself.

Watching For Warning Signs

Each of these mind control techniques can be dangerous on their own, but when more than one technique is combined then things can quickly spiral out of control. Talented manipulators are experts at starting small and slowly building up, turning up the intensity while adding in new techniques until their control over their target becomes complete.

This is why you must always be vigilant, constantly looking out for any signs of these mind control techniques. You shouldn't be quick to dismiss gut reactions. If you ignore the first warning signs, it can become easier to miss the other red flags that may come along. Scenarios that start out innocently can quickly spiral out of control when you are dealing with a masterful manipulator.

The best time to break free from a manipulator's grasp is in the earliest phases of their mind control efforts. Shaking yourself loose from control during the early stages is a relatively simple thing when compared to the monumental effort required to break free from a developed and layered mind control regime.

Don't let things get out of control. Keep an eye out for mind control and act quickly when you believe you're being targeted.

Chapter 3:
The Infamous Dark Triad

"Always treat everyone with respect. You never know who is secretly a psychopath."

— Alex Wayne

Both history books and works of literary fiction are filled with dark but compelling characters. Judged by purely moral standards they should be characters of pure loathing, but yet there's something that attracts them to us. While these darkly attractive characters have many different characteristics, modern science has pointed the way to three particular traits that are especially powerful, and dangerous.

The Dark Triad. It sounds like a criminal organization from a work of fiction, but it's a psychological concept that is all too real. While the different traits have gone by various names over the ages, publications like Psychology Today have defined the three as psychopathy, narcissism, and Machiavellianism. These three traits are powerful on their own, but when they're combined in an individual they can be earth shattering.

If you want to understand the nature of power, then you need to understand these three attributes. Knowing what to look for is the first step towards being able to defend yourself from their pull. But be warned, even those who understand the theory of dark psychology can still find themselves becoming hypnotized by the talents of a Dark Triad individual. Dealing with them is like interacting with a wild animal. The moment you get too comfortable with them is the moment when they're most likely to strike.

The Holy Grail of Dark Psychology

The study of dark psychology could be said to be the study of the Dark Triad. This is because the Dark Triad has been around much longer than the science of psychology, or any science for that matter. The Dark Triad arises from human nature, the science of our brains, and the natural neurodiversity that accounts for the many personality types that exist.

There have likely been Dark Triad individuals for as long as humans have been walking upright and speaking in full sentences. These individuals were given the natural talent and aptitude for manipulating their fellow humans, while the innocents around them didn't have the tools necessary to see just what was being done to them. Fortunately, we now live in an age where the triad has been identified and defined. Still, it takes careful study and practice to recognize the most subtle Dark Triad individuals, and it requires even more to learn how to harness the power for your own purposes.

Dark psychology has developed so that individuals who don't possess Dark Triad traits can develop the skills and understanding that come naturally to those born into the Dark Triad.

Deciphering the Traits

So far we've been discussing the Dark Triad as a whole, but if you wish to fully understand the phenomenon then you must look at each of the individual traits. It's similar to the way that we talk about the US government as a single entity even though it is divided into the executive, judicial, and legislative branches. And as with the government, further subdivisions can be made as you dig deeper into the subject. But to begin with, we must take time to carefully define narcissism, Machiavellianism, and psychopathy as individual traits.

Narcissism

First is narcissism. This trait is usually defined as a pathological level of self-interest. The term was coined in 1898 by British writer and scientist Haelock Ellis (Rhodewalt).

The word narcissism comes from the Greek mythology's Narcissus. The character was so famously vain that he was said to have fallen in love with his own reflection. What many people don't realize is that this is just part of the story. Narcissus was famed for his beauty, and it didn't only charm the man himself. Greek Mythology is filled with characters who fall in love with Narcissus and do whatever it takes to try and earn his affection in return. Each of these stories ends tragically, because as the reflection anecdote suggestions, the only person Narcissus truly loved was himself.

The same goes for modern narcissists. These are individuals who are focused on themselves, to the exclusion of all of those around them.

Narcissistic Traits

- Inflated opinion of themselves
- High level of entitlement
- Envy of those who possess things that they feel they deserve
- Belief that they belong to a superior class of people
- Never ending demands for special attention
- A constant need to control conversations
- Lack of empathy for others
- Inability to handle criticism, no matter how small
- Borrows from others without making any attempt to pay back debts
- Gets upset when others bring attention to outstanding debts
- Able to hold grudges for long periods of time
- Constantly looking to "upgrade" to bigger and better things
- A pathological need to put others down in order to elevate themselves
- Emotionally charged reactions to failures, both real and perceived

("Narcissistic personality disorder", 2017)

The simple way to understand narcissists is that they believe the world revolves around them. But please understand that it goes beyond ordinary selfishness.

The narcissist plays on the fact that most people do not recognize that they aren't playing by the normal rules. Normal human relations are based on a sense of give and take, where charity and kindness from one party is rewarded by reciprocal behavior from the other. Narcissists are more than willing to receive gifts, but they don't feel the natural compulsion to return the favor. Still, the skilled narcissist learns how to lead on others, convincing them that great rewards are within reach. They will extract all that they can from an individual before abandoning them once a better opportunity arises.

Machiavellianism

Next comes Machiavellianism. Those with this trait are prone to strategically lying to others to exploit them. The trait was identified by American social psychologists Richard Christie and Florence L. Geis.

This trait is the least well known, but you might recognize the name given the fact that its namesake has been quoted previously in this book. It is named after Niccolò Machiavelli, the Italian political philosopher who is infamous for his book *The Prince*. In that book, Machiavelli instructed rulers on how to lead using deception and subterfuge, behavior that naturally arises in Machiavellian individuals. The term was a purely political term until it was brought into the realm of the social sciences by Christie and Geis in their 1970 book *Studies in Machiavellianism* (Blundell, 2015).

Machiavellian traits

- Highly ambitious
- Fixated on power and profit above all else
- Quick to give strategic complements
- Willing to harm others to achieve their goals
- Unapologetic about the negative consequences of their actions
- Highly cynical

- Slow to make serious commitments and quick to break them

(Blundell, 2015)

One of the things that makes Machiavellian individuals so dangerous is the fact that they are more in touch with normal individuals than many narcissists and psychopaths. They don't ignore the needs of others, they use them to suit their own purposes. While other low-empathy individuals are quick to burn down bridges, a Machiavellian will build as many bridges as they need to in order to get where they want to be. It's only after they've reached their goal that they will turn on those who helped them get where they were going.

Psychopathy

The final point of the triad is psychopathy. This trait is defined by a pathological level of indifference towards others.

Psychopathic Traits

- Exaggerated sense of self esteem
- Lying as a force of habit, even when unnecessary
- Prone to risky and unpredictable behavior
- Lack of concern for the wellbeing of others
- Difficulty or inability to imagine the thoughts and emotions of others
- Prone to engage in risky sexual acts
- Inability to recognize responsibility for their actions
- Driven to leech off of others with no regard to the cost
- Fantastic and unrealistic ideas of the future
- Need for constant stream of activity
- Inability to maintain a long-term romantic relationship

- History of criminal behavior
- A seemingly natural, if superficial, appeal or magnetism

("Everything You Wanted to Know About the Science of Psychopaths", 2018)

The most fundamental, and the most dangerous trait, a psychopath has is their lack of empathy. In the most severe cases a psychopath literally cannot imagine what others are feeling or thinking. When they look into the eyes of another human being they feel something similar to what the average person feels when looking into the eyes of an ant. You know there is something going on behind the eyes, but you can't really say what.

Nature Versus Nurture

When discussing any psychological traits, whether they belong to the Dark Triad or not, the question arises whether people are born with them or develop them over time.

The truth is that as of writing there is no clear answer. The human mind is a complex thing. Its complexity is beyond the most powerful supercomputer and the complex series of electrical pulses that goes on inside of our brains is impossible to fully observe at this time.

There are all sorts of opinions with regards to how traits like these come about. But the general consensus is that they are the result of a mix of genetic pre-programming and environmental influences. No one chooses the way their mind thinks, but that doesn't mean that people can't work to take control of their thought processes and guide them in a more productive way.

For those that suffer from extreme cases of narcissism, Machiavellianism, or psychopathy, this means that there is a chance that through therapy and hard work a healthier mental state can be achieved. But it also means that individuals who don't naturally show high levels of these traits can work to develop them. They may never be able to kill off their genetically programmed concern for what others think, but with practice it can be dulled.

Working in Combination

You now have a working knowledge of the different traits of the Dark Triad. Each of them can be dangerous on their own, but they are nothing compared to the threat that arises once the different traits are combined.

Can Dark Triad Traits Make you More Successful?

It's important to understand that each trait of the Dark Triad exists on a continuum. It's common for people to show signs of these traits from time to time throughout their life. Individuals who are purely psychotic and those with absolutely no psychotic traits are both uncommon.

For example, Machiavellianism is diagnosed using a test that assigns people a score between 0 and 100. Individuals who score 0 have absolutely no Machiavellian traits, while those who score 100 are purely Machiavellian. Almost no one scores 100, but that doesn't mean you can let your guard down. A score of 60 or higher qualifies an individual as a "high Machiavellian." Such individuals can be among the most dangerous (Blundell, 2015).

Those who possess Dark Triad traits in their purest forms are definitely dangerous, but they're also relatively easy to identify and avoid. It's the individuals with a more mixed personality that can be the most dangerous. They aren't so far gone that they can't blend in with the crowd, but even though they might act like everyone else, they are capable of powerful acts of manipulation.

If you looked at a list of the most successful leaders in the world of business and politics, you would be hard pressed to find someone who wasn't at least slightly Machiavellian.

Traits like psychopathy are more of a double-edged sword. Psychopaths don't care what other people think about them, which can be incredibly freeing. Anyone who wants to achieve anything in this world will have to be able to push through the haters and detractors who will try to shoot them down. The fact that psychopaths can honestly say that they don't care what others think is a distinct advantage in this area. But the danger comes when it's time to build a team to work towards a goal. No one can reach the highest levels of success on their own, but complete psychopaths can find it very difficult to build and manage teams.

So while possessing some degree of Dark Triad traits may provide certain advantages, there can also be extreme drawbacks if the traits are pushed beyond what normal people can tolerate. It's important to remember that the geniuses who are famous for misbehaving only got away with their poor behavior because of their genius. If the average person starts to act like an absolute maniac, they're more likely to get fired than given control of a Fortune 500 company.

Nevertheless, a temptation still exists. When you look at the success stories that are told about individuals who fall within the Dark Triad, all sorts of emotions rise up.

The first is a wave of fear and revulsion at the idea that such people walk among us. The second is a desire to gain the power these traits seem to offer.

There is no need to berate yourself if you feel like you could benefit from any of the traits we're discussing. It's a natural impulse. What really matters is what you do with your impulses.

The first thing to understand is that actually developing the sort of Dark Triad traits that can be clinically diagnosed might be impossible and is definitely ill-advised.

Still, you can model your behavior after people who do possess Dark Triad traits. The person who can channel these traits actually has an additional level of power because they gain some of their power without submitting to their mercy. People who naturally possess these traits often manipulate compulsively. This is just as likely to be damaging and destructive as it is empowering. For every Dark Triad individual that you see in positions of power and respect, there is another that is living in the gutters of society.

Manipulation can be a dangerous game. If you don't want to lose it all, then you need to keep a tight rein on your behavior. Learn how to emulate Dark Triad individuals while appreciating the fact that you'll never truly be like them. It might feel like a limitation, but it can actually be empowering.

Before you can control anyone else, you must first take control of yourself.

Chapter 4:
The Dark Side of Persuasion

"Manipulation, fueled with good intent, can be a blessing. But when used wickedly, it is the beginning of a magician's karmic calamity."

- T.F. Hodge

If you want to enjoy productive relationships with other human beings, then you either need to learn the art of persuasion or convince yourself that you are happy with whatever other people have in mind for you.

But while the act of persuasion itself can be natural and healthy, that doesn't mean that it can't take dark turns. Persuasion is like any other human endeavor. It can come in many different varieties. The form it takes tends to depend on the person practicing it. That's why you should always be cautious when faced with someone trying to persuade you to see things their way. They could have pure intentions, or they could be trying to lead you down a dark path.

Not All Persuasions Are Created Equal

When differentiating between normal behavior and behavior driven by dark psychology, there are a variety of things to consider, but they all build on the idea that dark psychology is self-centered. Manipulators put themselves first and will do whatever it takes to achieve the results they are after, even if it means hurting other people to make their dreams come true.

Still, it is hard to judge a complex suggestion based on this criteria. That's why we'll be looking at questions you can ask to see whether you are dealing with normal persuasion or something more sinister.

Judging Plans Based on Results

Who benefits from the suggestion?

If someone is trying to convince you to take a certain set of actions, you need to take the time to think about the full consequences of these actions. A plan that might seem honest and noble might turn out to have dangerous consequences down the line. This is especially important when dealing with potential manipulators, because they will often attempt to hide or downplay the risks and dangers of their plan. They don't want people to have the full truth, they only want to divulge information that might help them achieve their goals.

It also helps to look at the consequences of the plan being offered up. The normal persuader will try and bring plans to the table where everyone involved can benefit. Think about your average business, where the boss makes money, the employees get paid, and the customers get a good or service that they are happy with.

This is the sort of arrangement that society is built on, where everyone can get what they need and walk away satisfied.

A dark manipulator won't truly be concerned about spreading the wealth around. Their main goals are all self-centered, and everyone else is secondary. This is why manipulators are likely to come up with plans that are win-lose rather than win-win. Think about your average scam. They look like win-win situations at first, but as time goes by the mark realizes that they have been taken and will never see the rewards that they were promised.

Honesty

Do you believe the person you're talking to is being honest with you?

Every plan has risks and rewards. Even something as simple as your morning commute involves a certain level of risk. One thing that separates honest persuaders from dark manipulators is honesty when it comes to the topic of risks.

Honest persuaders are more up-front about the potential drawbacks of their suggestions. If they know they are asking someone to take a risky course of action, they will let them know about the risks in advance and do what they can to try and either minimize the risks or make the task worth the dangers involved.

A dark manipulator will not be honest about how risky their suggestions are. If they feel they must be honest for legal purposes, then they may mention the risks in an offhand manner or cram them into the fine print of a document. They won't take the time to make sure that the dangers are clear during the persuasion process. They don't care about the wellbeing of the person they are trying to persuade, they are only interested in getting what they desire.

Emotional Appeal

Is the suggestion based on logic or emotion?

There's no way around it—emotion is important in all human interactions. But that doesn't mean that the level of emotion involved doesn't change from one situation to another. Honest suggestions can involve appeals to emotions, but some level of restraint will be involved. No decent person wants to feel like they are emotionally blackmailing someone into following their suggestion.

Manipulators are different. They are used to controlling others by pressing emotional buttons. They won't hesitate to use guilt and other strong emotions to try and force people to go along with their plans. This is what makes manipulators especially dangerous. Their lack of shame allows them to go to extremes that most people are ill-equipped to deal with.

How to Recognize a Dark Persuader?

The scariest thing about dark persuaders is the fact that they can't be spotted at a glance. You need to get up close and personal before you can diagnose someone as a truly dangerous manipulator. But the closer you get to them, the greater the threat they might pose.

This is why you must always approach potential manipulators carefully. Keep your eyes peeled as you search for signs that they might be attempting to use you for their own personal gain.

Dishonesty

You should never ignore a lie. One of the biggest red flags that someone isn't what they seem is a stated falsehood. This doesn't mean that everyone that gets their facts mixed up is out to get you, but it does mean that if you catch someone telling you something that they know for a fact is false, then you should keep an eye on them.

If you are like most people, you have been taught to be forgiving. You might also let people slide because it's easier that way. But don't let this approach lead you to destruction. No lie is too small to ignore, and the smaller lies can actually be the most condemning. If someone is willing to lie about things that don't seem to mean anything at all, then who is to say that they aren't lying to you about truly important matters?

Dark manipulation is all about deception. The problem is that skilled manipulators generally have a good idea of what their targets do and do not know. The most talented stick to lying about things that their targets can't know. Still, eventually there will come a time when a lie gets told that the target is capable of seeing through.

A single lie can be like a loose thread. It might not seem like much, but if you start tugging at it, eventually everything can unravel.

A Shallow Social Life

You can learn a lot about someone by looking at the company they keep. That's why it helps to meet someone's friends and family before getting involved with them in a business or romantic relationship. Those people will be able to let you know how the person in question is when times get rough.

If you meet someone who has no family to speak of or close friends, then you might consider that as a red flag. While many people go through tragic times that strip them of close connections, it's also true that manipulators tend to drive away the people who are closest to them. You shouldn't immediately run away from someone just because they won't introduce you to their family, but such behavior is reason enough to look out for any other red flags that might pop up.

Selfishness

Another key element of dark psychology is its selfish nature. The dark persuader's goals are all centered around themselves. Everyone else is just a pawn to be used to achieve the manipulator's goal.

Still, do not think that recognizing this selfishness will be easy. Skilled manipulators know that they have to hide their self-centered nature in order to achieve their goals. They will often overcompensate for this weakness by parading about as a person of charity and goodwill. But these displays are often shallow, putting an emphasis on the appearance of charity rather than on actually helping anyone.

Pay close attention to how potential manipulators behave when you give or lend them something. Watch their eyes for a light of true appreciation, and see if they try and return the favor at any time. Be especially alert for signs of entitlement.

Defensiveness

One way that you can test to see whether or not you can trust a person is by asking them tough but honest questions. While few people enjoy answering such questions, honest and empathetic individuals will do what they can to answer them honestly and thoroughly.

With this being said, you should also remember that not all manipulators are alike. While some are highly impulsive and prone to unrealistic thinking, others are more meticulous when weaving their plots. These individuals can be prepared for questioning and may be able to give answers that are more impressive than an honest person's. After all, they might not be sweating since they aren't worried about hurting others the way that most people are.

This is why you can't just look for one particular trait when trying to determine whether or not someone is a manipulator.

Outsider Skepticism

The dark persuader is skilled in controlling the minds of the people they come into contact with, but even the most talented manipulators will eventually have to deal with limitations. The manipulator must actively pull the wool over the eyes of individuals, because those that see the situation objectively rather than through the lens created by the manipulator will be able to see the flaws in their plan.

Have you ever wondered why it's so easy for you to recognize when your friends have chosen the wrong romantic partners, while it's almost impossible for them to quickly see their own mistakes? This is because interpersonal relationships make it difficult to see clearly. We are hard-wired for relationships, and once an emotional link has been established, the logical mind loses a lot of its control.

This means that if you want to get a more objective idea of what you're dealing with you should seek outside help. You should also try your hardest to listen to outside input, even when it's painful to hear. While it will be tempting to tell them that they don't understand because they don't really know the person in question, the reality is that their distance is what allows them to see things for what they really are.

If your friends and family are telling you that someone seems like a manipulator, then you need to step back and seriously consider whether or not they might be a dark persuader. The more you fear what the answer to this line of questioning is, the more essential it is that you pursue it.

Fundamental Dark Persuasion Techniques

If you want to live a safe and happy life, you must always be on the lookout for dark manipulators. You can never really be sure where they might show up. The sad truth is that sometimes manipulators can hide the darkness inside for years at a time, only revealing their true nature when they feel that they have to. This is why you must try and limit the times when you let your guard down.

The best way to defend yourself is by recognizing manipulators before they can gain any sort of hold on you. The best way to do this is by familiarizing yourself with the basic dark persuasion techniques. If you witness someone around you using these techniques on you or someone else, then you should be extremely wary of that individual.

Frog Boiling

How do you boil a frog alive?

Sounds like the sort of question that only a psychopath would ask, but that means it's an appropriate question given the topic.

If most people are given such a chance, they will treat it like most cooking projects and start by bringing the water to a boil before tossing the frog into the pot. The problem is that the frog will react violently to the drastic change in temperature.

The real way to boil a frog is to put it in a room-temperature pot and then slowly increase the temperature. The frog's body will slowly adjust to the changes, allowing it to stay in the water even as it reaches extreme temperatures that it would never have gotten into willingly. By the time the frog notices the dangerous heat it's too late, they can no longer escape, and are boiled alive.

At least, that's how the story goes. Whether or not frogs actually behave that way, the concept stands. People can be taken to insane places if you pull them along gradually. That is why the most dangerous manipulators know that sometimes they have to work in slow, subtle, and gradual steps to get some people to do what they want them to do.

This sort of behavior is commonly seen in cults, where new members are often invited under the pretense that the cult is a non-religious organization or a denomination of a more mainstream religion. The more unique beliefs of the organization are then revealed gradually, so that the convert has time to process and accept each new concept individually.

By the time that the true nature of the manipulator is revealed it's already too late, the target has been boiled alive.

Imminent Rewards That Never Arrive

People can overlook a lot of things if they believe that they will be rewarded for their faith. Manipulators take advantage of this fancy by using promises of future rewards to extract resources from their targets. The problem is that while they might constantly tell people that they are just a matter of days away from success, those days never seem to really pass. Days turn into weeks, weeks turn into months, and all the manipulator has to show for themselves is a new set of excuses

The rewards that a manipulator promises a target are like the carrots dangled in front of a donkey by a cart driver. The donkey is meant to think that they are always just a step away from their big reward, but the fact is that if they actually got their reward then they would cease being useful to the person controlling them. That's why the carrot is always being moved along with the donkey, so that the donkey will never actually get the carrot and will instead keep pulling the cart.

The manipulator is the same way with their promises. Something big is always just around the corner, they only need a little more money, support, or time before they can finally hit the jackpot and make everyone rich and famous.

You might think that the manipulator wouldn't be able to keep such a scam going on for very long, but you should know that the longer a human goes along with a scam, the harder it is to break the spell. This is because of something known as the sunk cost fallacy. The idea is that the more you can get someone to invest into an idea or project, the harder it will be for them to abandon the effort even if it is clearly failing.

People do not want to admit that they have wasted their time and resources because such an admission would make the loss "real." As long as they can pretend as if a big payday is just around the corner, they don't have to worry about their expenses because they'll make everything back plus interest on their day of triumph.

The only problem is that with dark persuaders, that triumph never comes. They will bleed their targets dry until they decide to move on toward greener pastures or are forced to move on. Either way, those that they targeted are left dealing with greater losses than they would have suffered if they had been able to bite the bullet at the first sign of trouble and admit that the plan wasn't going to work.

Secrecy

The light can reveal many things that the dark manipulator would prefer to keep hidden. This is why they tend to work in secrecy, limiting the spread of information and encouraging targets to keep things within the group.

A manipulator will explain that the relationship they have with their target is special. It's so special that others wouldn't understand. Telling outsiders would just invite ridicule or spread the secret around so that it loses some of its potency. With all this in mind, they'll explain that their target must be quiet about the sacred details of their relationship. Letting them out could lead to disaster.

That last statement is powerful because it is partially true. Outsiders can destroy these sorts of relationships, but most would argue that such destructions are actually positive.

The fact is that outsiders are able to catch things that people who are closer to the manipulator might miss. Since an outsider isn't living through the intimate moments of the process, they are able to look at things more objectively. An honest talk with a friend could alert the target to the fact that the manipulator's statements don't make sense or are unrealistic, and without the manipulator to act as a slick apologist their arguments can fall apart.

This is why dark persuaders will do everything they can to keep things as secretive as possible. They will often try and develop secrecy and social cohesion simultaneously by emphasizing that the target now belongs to a special group that outsiders are incapable of understanding.

If you want to avoid manipulation, then one of the best things you can do is to cultivate an open and honest group of friends you can discuss matters with. Their second opinion might save you from disaster.

Chapter 5:
CEM - Covert Emotional Manipulation

"Half of the people lie with their lips; the other half with their tears."

- Nassim Nicholas Taleb

Every form of manipulation can be dangerous, but it's possible that no method is more frightening or upsetting than emotional manipulations. Our emotions sit at the core of our being, tied to the most sacred elements of our lives. The idea that some stranger might use our deepest feelings against us can be too much to bear, but it is something we need to face head on.

Dark persuaders do not respect the sanctity of human emotions. The fact that we can have such a complicated relations with our emotions only encourages them to turn them into weapons. If you only learn to look out for one form of manipulation, then you should definitely come to understand covert emotional manipulation. It's a topic that you simply can't afford to ignore.

Purest Form of Manipulation

The first line of defense against manipulation is the logical mind. If we can think a situation through carefully and clearly, then we can usually come up with some sort of logical solution. We might not be able to pull it off, but we're still able to plan it out.

This all goes out the window when emotions are involved.

Think of our emotions as the secret backdoor that is installed into our being. It allows people to bypass the vast majority of our mental defenses and go directly for our most central and vulnerable areas.

Simply put, emotions tend to be the weak spot for every human being. This is the reason why the worst villains know to target the family members of someone they wish to control. The emotional ties between loved ones are so strong that they can be used to convince people to do things they would never do otherwise.

While you might never be in a situation where people you care about are kidnapped and used against you, you will almost certainly find yourself in situations where people are working in secret to convince you to take a certain action. You may be under the control of a manipulator as you read this. The truly scary thing about covert emotional manipulation is the fact that it is carried out in secret.

To understand covert emotional manipulation, the concept must be broken apart so that each individual element can be examined.

The first word is covert, which means secret or concealed. This helps us understand that we are dealing with a behavior that is not for public consumption. Manipulators who engage in covert emotional manipulation are trying to fly under the radar and avoid detection by their target and anyone else who might threaten their efforts.

The next word is emotional. This means that we're talking about manipulation that is focused on emotions like fear, love, anger, disgust, nostalgia, and all of the rest. This type of manipulation is diving deep, going beyond logic and reason and digging into the soft and vulnerable core within all of our hearts. Emotional attacks can feel just as painful as physical assaults, but emotional attacks aren't necessarily illegal. Skilled emotional manipulators can do incredible damage without ever having to face the music for their vicious actions.

Finally, the last word in the term is manipulation. As stated earlier in this book, this term refers to actions where one party is trying to control the other for their own personal needs. It's about reducing a human being into something like a tool to be used and tossed away.

When you add together all of these elements, it's easy to see why covert emotional manipulation is the most destructive form of manipulation in addition to being the purest.

And if that wasn't bad enough, it's also one of the hardest things to get away from.

The fact is that every human interaction has an emotional level. You're happy to see your friends and sad when they leave. You're scared to speak in front of a crowd but excited when you get up and find that you can hold their attention. Emotions are an essential part of the human existence, with us every moment of our waking lives.

This constant presence is one of the reasons why emotionally manipulative actions can go unnoticed. People who are used to dealing with a constant emotional flux may not immediately pick up on some of the more subtle attempts at emotional control.

Skilled manipulators can carefully read the room and adjust their emotional overtures so that they manage the flow of the situation without drawing attention to their actions. It can actually be quite amazing to watch if you aren't one of the poor souls who has been caught up in the magic show and dragged along wherever the manipulator is taking them.

Can't Escape From It

The fact of the matter is that no matter where you go and what scenario you find yourself in, you will always be at risk of some form of emotional manipulation. It might be at the hands of a dark persuader, or you could be dealing with an individual who is simply damaged and is taking out their own issues on innocent individuals such as yourself.

Your relationship with your boss, the friendships you have with your peers, the loving bonds you share with your romantic partner, and the deep familial connections you share with your blood relatives. All of these connections are emotional in their own ways, although some are more emotional than others. This means that each of these relationships could go badly if just one person decides to take the relationship you have and turn it into a weapon that might force you to submit to their will.

You may not want to believe that those who are closest to you may turn out to be manipulators, but it is more likely than any of us would like to admit. As the saying goes, we hurt the ones that we love. Some of the most damaging and protracted cases of manipulation involve close family members. The bond between a mother and child might be the most sacred thing in existence, and yet the papers are filled with stories of horrific conflicts between parents and children that end in tragedy.

Simply put, it's a dangerous world. You can't even know you're safe when you're around your family.

Still, there's a point where you can get too paranoid. If you've never had any issues with your mother before, then chances are she is not using dark psychology to manipulate you into behaving in horrific ways. Nevertheless, it's worth taking the time to develop the abilities necessary to see through the fronts that people put up and see what they are trying to slip by everyone else.

Consider this: every interaction offers a chance for manipulation. This is because even when our hearts are guarded, a skilled manipulator might be able to slide past our defenses and get to us. Still, we need to go about our lives. The fact of the matter is that since every interaction has some emotional layer, it can be difficult at first to decide who is trying to manipulate you emotionally and who is just engaging with you on a natural and human level.

Consider this: even an individual who is highly skilled in the mysteries of dark psychology will find it hard to generate the sort of intense emotions that a completely innocent first date might bring about.

This is why it's so important to remember just what makes dark psychology dark—the intent. Dark persuaders are malicious and self-centered. If they work to make you feel happy or loved, it is only so that you will do something for them in return. They aren't interested in you as an emotional being with love and desires that are all your own, they only see you as a tool that they can use to achieve their own goals.

So how do you find out which individuals are practicing this dangerous and vile form of manipulation? Careful observation and research.

Watch how they act around you and keep track of how they make you feel. If you feel your emotions shifting as they make subtle changes to their tone, posture, or word choice, then they might be casting a metaphorical spell on you. It's also important to watch and see if they try and use this power to try and get you to take some action.

Dark manipulation is all about getting people to take actions that are not in their own interest. The manipulator turns their target into an extension of themselves, puppets who exist to serve the master pulling their strings. It's a terrible fate.

It's horrifying to watch a skilled emotional manipulator at work, observing as they tug on heart strings and force their targets to dance. But what's even more horrifying might be the fact that you yourself may be manipulating others emotionally without even realizing it.

Remember that emotional manipulation comes naturally to us as social creatures. The ability to tap into the emotions of others is practically essential for your survival as a human being and has been for countless generations, so don't be surprised if you discover that you've been unknowingly pressuring those around you using strong and subtle emotions.

One of the most difficult parts of dealing with covert emotional manipulation is striking a healthy balance. While it's definitely important to look out for potential manipulation, you also can't get so paranoid that it destroys your ability to live a healthy and productive life. There have been many cases where people become their own worst enemies, doubting those closest to them and isolating themselves. The irony is once isolation has occurred, it's easy to long for real human connections, and that longing will once again open them up to the threat of manipulation.

The past is the past, what is important is the future. You may not be able to cut yourself off completely from the emotional manipulators of the world, but you can take steps to limit the impact they have on you.

Common Techniques

Human emotions are complex things. This means that there are many different approaches that a manipulator can take if they want to mess with someone's emotions. Other manipulation techniques that we've looked at can be emotionally charged, but strategies that we are about to examine are some of the most emotionally potent tools in a manipulator's arsenal.

Emotional Conditioning

If you've ever heard of Pavlov's dogs, then you understand the basics of conditioning. To sum the story up, a Russian scientist named Ivan Pavlov discovered that when dogs heard a specific sound before each and every feeding time, they eventually began to drool when the sound was played, even if no food was present. This shows how the mind can create connections between certain external stimuli and physio-emotional reactions.

Think about it this way. Pavlov learned to rewire the minds of dogs using only a metronome and some food. The human mind might be larger and more complex than a canine mind, but the basic principles remain the same. The human mind can be conditioned, and manipulators will abuse this fact.

Consider a patient and focused manipulator who carefully withholds all positive emotions until a certain condition is met. They might want to train their partner to cook dinner for them, so they begin to withhold things like love and affection until after a meal has been cooked. This creates a sense of conditioning in the mind of the target where suddenly cooking for their partner is closely tied with the positive emotions that swirl around displays of affection.

This is just one broad example to help illustrate the concept. A skilled manipulator can create all sorts of conditioned reactions by carefully managing their behavior. The trick is that the manipulator is cold and detached, while the person being manipulated has to deal with the natural emotions of love, envy, withdrawal, and longing. When emotional imbalances like this exist, it is all too easy for amoral individuals to take advantage of the situation.

Divide and Conquer

While many emotional manipulation strategies are based around one-on-one interactions, the more advanced manipulators will be able to leverage larger social groups to help control the emotional state of their target. Instead of focusing on one individual alone, they will go after their target and people close to their target.

The name of the game is divide and conquer. This term was originally invented to refer to the strategy that Imperial powers like Great Britain would use to take control of populous nations. A British officer in command of a thousand soldiers understood that even with their technological advantages they couldn't control a nation of millions on their own. So they enlisted the help of the locals to colonize the locals. The idea was that the existing divisions between different ethnic groups, religions, and other population groups could be exploited. If Hindus and Muslims were busy worrying over one another, then they would be unprepared to handle the British colonizers that were slowly taking control.

The days of Britain's global empire are now long gone, but their insidious logic still stands. A skilled manipulator can take advantage of group dynamics by looking for divisions within the group and exacerbating them, driving them apart so that they'll never ally against their common enemy.

Watch out for manipulators that act like aloof and impartial third-party observers while seeking out and spreading gossip. Manipulators understand that a few juicy pieces of gossip can turn friends to enemies, and drive people into the arms of those who are seen as good listeners. A manipulator might seem to be an attentive listener, but that's only because they are carefully searching for any detail that they can use to further their goals.

Heightened Dramatics

The worst manipulators tend to be individuals who have emotional issues, but different people experience such issues in different ways. While some manipulators are quite cold and unemotional themselves, others may go off in the opposite direction.

Some particularly self-centered manipulators will seek out or generate dramatic events so that they can be the center of attention. They see the world as a stage, and they are starring in the leading role. If they can't have all eyes on them, then they start to fall apart, creating an even more dramatic situation.

In addition to playing the role of an actor, the manipulator will also act as a director and cast those around them in their dramatics. Sometimes they will just use them to generate even more drama, but the more Machiavellian individuals will orchestrate the drama so that it helps them achieve their greater goals.

As humans we are naturally drawn to the dramatic. It's the reason why we love movies, television, books, and the theater. It's all too easy to get swept up in the dramatics of a talented manipulator, so make sure to be on your guard against individuals who constantly have the drama dial cranked up to 11.

Projection

You should always pay special attention to accusations made by potential manipulators. The words they use may be the key to understanding where exactly they are coming from.

This is because one behavior that is common along manipulators and Dark Triad individuals is projection. This is where an individual projects their own emotional baggage onto the person they are talking to. For example, a cheater might handle their feelings of guilt by accusing their partner of cheating.

With this in mind, if you pay attention to accusations an accuser makes against you, then you can get a decent picture of what is going on in their mind. Just turn the accusations around and ask yourself whether or not things make more sense with the tables turned.

It should be noted that you have to approach the idea of projection carefully. It's a powerful tool for understanding human psychology, but it can quickly get out of hand. If you find yourself accusing everyone around you of projection, then it might be that you yourself are the one projecting. This is why you need to be careful about the conclusions you jump to and very self-critical when considering your own feelings.

Chapter 6:

Mind Games or

Psychological Warfare?

"In the big leagues everyone has ability. It always comes down to mind games. Who ever is more mentally strong-wins."

- Muhammad Ali

The term "mind games" can be difficult to take seriously at first because the name has an almost playful connotation. After all, who doesn't like to play games? But this is precisely what can make mind games so dangerous. Anyone who has wrestled with a sibling knows that the line between play fighting and actual fighting is thin. Even if neither party is trying to hurt the other, all it takes is one miscalculation to inflict pain and suffering.

Now imagine that one of the individuals involved has malicious intent.

The problem with mind games in the dark psychology sense is the disconnect between the two parties involved. The person being targeted is playing by the normal rules of human society and is limited by things like empathy and a sense of right and wrong. The dark persuader often operates without these restrictions. The only thing written in their rulebook is that there are no rules.

They will do whatever it takes to win.

They Aren't Really Games, Are They?

When do games become something more?

Imagine finding yourself in a fencing match. You might be a little nervous if you've never taken part in such a game before, but you won't be too nervous because you know that fencing is a safe activity. The person across from you looks like they know what they are doing and has a relaxed attitude that puts your mind at ease. Everything fits with your preconceived notions, and so your critical thinking shuts down so you can follow the steps you're expected to take.

But once the match starts, something starts to feel off. Your opponent is going through the motions you'd expect, but there is an edge to him that feels like it doesn't belong in the game you've agreed to take part in. Still, your first few exchanges of lunges and parries goes as you'd expect, and in the rush of the moment you get so caught up with moving from moment to moment that you lose sight of the bigger picture.

It's only when you feel a stinging in your side that you realize something is wrong.

You look down and see that your opponent's foil has drawn blood. He's not using the blunted blade that the rules call for, he's using a real weapon that has just done real harm.

Looking up, you see that his expression is unchanged. He looks calm and in control. His demeanor is so commanding that you start to question your own.

As you deal with your confusion your opponent is able to capitalize on your weakness. He slices through your guard and cuts you to ribbons. By the time you realize it's not a game, it's too late. You're lying bleeding on the floor.

This scenario may seem outlandish, but it is an accurate depiction of the damage a dark persuader can do with mind games. You never know just how dangerous a game can be until you play it with someone who is willing to do whatever is necessary to win. You quickly learn that any sport can be a blood sport when approached with a dark mindset.

More Than a Game

One frightening thing about dealing with a true manipulator is their vastly different values. The things that an individual with a Dark Triad personality values may be similar to the things a normal person values in some superficial ways, but there are also dramatic differences that can lead to disastrous consequences.

To begin with, just about every human being has a desire to come out on top in competitions. No one plays a game to lose. But while most normal humans are willing to accept defeat, individuals with Dark Triad traits abhor defeat and will do whatever it takes to win. This means they will take extreme measures that others would never think of, treating even simple games as life or death struggles that must end with the total annihilation of their opponents.

Another cause for concern is the fact that you may not understand the true extent of an individual's darkness until you've already gotten deep into a competition. Dark manipulators often learn how to fake basic human emotions. It's only when situations start to get more drastic that the cracks in their armor start to show. This is another reason why it is so important that you develop the ability to recognize manipulators as soon as possible. The best way to win a mind game with a dark influencer is by avoiding it in the first place.

Still, not all conflicts can be avoided. There are some games we are forced into playing, so it's worth looking deeper into the dark psychology of mind games.

Three Mind Games We're All Guilty of Playing

One thing that you need to understand is that we all play mind games. Those who say they don't play such games either misunderstand what they are or suffer from some psychological blind spots. Mind games are a normal part of human psychology. And just like any other area of psychology, dark manipulators take what naturally exists and crank it up to extremes for their own purposes.

So if you want to understand mind games in the dark psychology context, then it's helpful to start at a more normal level. Once you recognize the games that you yourself might be playing on a daily basis, then you shouldn't have too much difficulty seeing how the dark manipulators we've been looking at throughout this book can twist and distort our minds in dangerous ways.

The Blame Game

No one wants to believe that they are at fault. Most people feel awful when they believe that they are the reason that something has gone wrong. That is why it's common for people to quickly pass the blame onto others, whether or not the other person deserves it.

The best way to live a happy and healthy life is to accept blame personally as soon as possible while taking your time when blaming others. This doesn't mean that you should automatically assume that everything is your fault and that you should trust anyone who says something is your fault. On the contrary, while you should learn to deal with your own feelings of personal responsibility, you should be slow to accept blame handed down by other people.

Even if the person you are interacting with seems to be making a good case for why you're at fault, you shouldn't just assume that they are acting from a positive place. Ask yourself whether they seem like they want to help you grow as an individual or whether they want to pass the blame along so they don't have to deal with it themselves?

Finally, you need to be prepared to accept the fact that Dark Triad individuals will almost never own up to their own actions. Even when they apologize they will often weave countless excuses and dodges into their apologies. "I'm sorry you feel that way," is a common call, appearing to accept responsibility while avoiding it in actuality.

You may be looking for a way to trick a manipulator into taking the blame for a problem they've caused, but down this road lies madness. What you need to be able to do is accept that even if they clearly are to blame they will never own up to it. You should also understand that certain personality types are pathologically unable to accept blame. Getting them to see their fault is like getting a colorblind individual to see all the colors of the rainbow.

Know when something isn't going to happen, accept it, and move on with your life.

Insult Humor

One of the things that sets mind games apart from other mind control and manipulation techniques is the ambiguity involved in. Many of the games operate along a razor-thin line separating healthy and unhealthy behavior. This can serve an important role in socializing individuals into larger society. Playing such games helps them calibrate themselves to the rules of society in general and the individual needs of those around them in particular. A clear example of this can be seen in the use of what we will call insult humor.

Insult humor is any sort of joke at the expense of another person. It can sound cruel when looked at in a clinical way, but anyone who has had a normal childhood has experienced times when they bonded with friends, family, and peers through the use of insult humor.

Properly used, insult humor can help peers to toughen up one another in a safe environment before they are thrust into more serious situations where they will need to withstand harsh criticism. It also serves as a type of bonding. The entire ritual is based on the idea that friends and family can say things to one another that no one would allow a stranger to say. This allows for criticisms to be aired in a more productive environment, with the humor acting like a spoonful of sugar to help the metaphorical medicine go down.

But while insult humor can be productive, it can also be destructive. There is a fine line between jokes that help to toughen someone up and jokes that tear them down. While normal individuals will try and adjust their jokes so that they don't cause lasting harm to their target, a manipulator will use these jokes to break down their target for their own purposes.

The modus operandi of a dark manipulator is breaking down individuals so that they can be built up according to the desires of the manipulator. This is disturbingly similar to the way that humor can be used to direct individuals into the path that society wishes them to follow, but we will focus on person-to-person manipulation now.

Sometimes it is easy to recognize when jokes have gotten too cruel, but some manipulators are so subtle that their jokes might seem acceptable to strangers who don't fully grasp the dynamics at play. With this in mind, it can sometimes be difficult to decide whether insult humor is constructive or destructive.

The easiest way to spot manipulative insult humor is by looking to see whether there is a balanced relationship. Does the person being insulted have the freedom to respond in kind? Many Dark Triad individuals have no problem pouring heinous insults on others but can't handle even the slightest amount of criticism. If someone in your life is constantly joking about you but can't take a joke about themselves, then you should know that they might be using humor to manipulate you.

Another thing to look for is how the jokes are targeted. Is the person making the jokes doing what they can to avoid particularly sensitive topics, or are they consistently targeting vulnerable areas? Manipulators are like predators, they know to target weak points and have a way of homing in on them with startling precision.

Having a sense of humor is important, but so is having a sense of self-respect. If someone is constantly joking about your shortcomings but can't take a joke themselves, then their presence may be hazardous to your mental health.

Gaslighting

The final game we will look at is also the most extreme. Gaslighting is a game people play by which they bring the other person's sanity or perception of reality into doubt (Sarkis, 2017). You may think that this is something you would never do, but before you give yourself a clean bill of health you need to ask yourself a question. Have you ever told someone they were crazy for having a different opinion than you?

There's no shame in admitting that you have. It's a common tactic that comes from a deep-seated place within us all. When we deal with people who have beliefs that come in direct conflict with our own, it's easy to look at the other person as crazy. Seeing things from their point of view is challenging, so of course we often resort to something as basic as name calling when faced with a claim that our minds can barely deal with.

As with most psychological threats, the danger comes when natural impulses are taken to extremes. Instead of simply calling the other person crazy, a manipulator will start to use all of their mental powers to try and convince them that there is something wrong with their mind. They will go beyond presentations of facts and logical arguments and start to use covert emotional manipulation to sow seeds of doubt.

While gaslighting can be dangerous even in its less severe forms, it's not hard to see how things can become particularly insidious when Dark Triad individuals are involved. Someone who is willing to do whatever it takes to win this game can go to great lengths to convince someone that not only are they wrong, but there is something wrong with their brain for holding the beliefs that they do. A true psychopath will see no harm in fabricating evidence to prove their position. They may also convince third parties to join in, so that their target feels social pressure to doubt their own memories and experiences.

If you believe that someone is attempting to gaslight you, then the best thing you can do is disengage. While it helps to gather up any evidence you can to support your own claims and beliefs, you should be careful about presenting such evidence to the manipulator. Instead of being convinced, they will take your evidence and try and find some way to use it against you, further weakening your own position and mental health.

It's especially important to watch out for signs of gaslighting in intimate relationships. When arguments occur over events that took place in private, then things can quickly become dicey. Mental abuse leaves no physical evidence and doesn't offer an opportunity for an objective third party to step in and set the record straight. This is why abusers can run so wild with gaslighting in relationships. As long as they maintain the emotional high ground, they can convince their partner to doubt their own memory and experience.

This is an evil and insidious form of behavior that everyone should be on the lookout for. If you start to catch a friend or partner lying to you about events that you remember clearly, especially instances of abuse or negative behavior, then you must instantly be on your guard. You might feel like you are jumping the gun, but the deeper you allow a manipulator to dig into your mind, the more difficult it will be to clean up the mess that they create.

And Many More

In this book we only have enough space to take a brief look at some of the mind games people play, but you should already understand how widespread the issue is and how quickly things can spiral out of control. Mind games are far from harmless in a world of dark manipulators. That's why it's worth taking the time to look around you and watch for the different mind games people around you are playing. Try to catch and label the different games, but what's even more important is paying attention to how different people play them.

If you catch someone in your life behaving ruthlessly in even simple exchanges, then you should expect them to behave even more ruthlessly when there are serious stakes involved. Watching how people handle little things will help you to predict how they handle the big things. Sometimes people will surprise you, but you shouldn't be so open-minded that you are blind to the realities in front of you. Dark manipulators have their eyes on you, watching how you behave and cataloging your actions for future reference. Don't allow others to gain an advantage over you. Act proactively to learn all you can about those around you.

Why Do We Play Them?

After learning how small and petty mind games can blow up into major disasters, you're probably wondering why we engage in such destructive behavior in the first place. Wouldn't life be easier if everyone could just be up front about how they feel and what they want?

The truth is that while the world might be a better place if human nature could be perfected, as of writing there doesn't seem to be any way to create perfection amidst the confusion and chaos of the real world. Human beings may have come a long way from our wild past, but we still carry the genes of the furry hunter-gatherers who spent nights huddled into the darkness while jungle cats hunted them for meat.

A Biological Imperative

The rules to the mind games we play aren't written in books, but on the very DNA that makes us human. This is another area of our behavior where you can't understand why we do the things we do in modern life without looking back to our ancient past. While scientists still have a variety of different theories on why human beings play mind games, you can look at mind games as mental reflections of the other games humans naturally play.

Human children learn to play fight as a way to let out aggression in a healthy and productive way. The children learn how to fight so that they can defend themselves from real threats in the future without having to face the danger of an actual threat. The skills learned are similar to practicing the real thing, but the stakes are lower and people are less likely to get truly hurt (Kelley & Kelley, 2018).

Mind games also evolved in the small communities of prehistoric humanity. Individuals needed to be mentally and emotionally tough in order to survive, but they also needed to maintain a certain level of peace within the tribe. Direct conflict could lead to permanent divisions and threaten the survival of the entire tribe, so individuals needed to find ways to flex their emotional muscles without threatening the tribe. Mind games developed as a way for people to address real needs and concerns without jumping into the sort of direct conflict that could quickly escalate into physical violence.

This theory means that mind games are pre-programmed into our mind. And as we'd expect in such a world, just about every human being plays mind games from time to time. This isn't something to be ashamed of, but it is something you need to be aware of. As we've established, there's a thin line between harmless games and pitched conflicts that can lead to lasting scars.

Mind games in general may be a natural part of life, but the sort of mind games played by manipulators are not healthy. You should always be on the lookout for attempts to lure you into dangerous games. To paraphrase a classic movie, when it comes to a manipulator's mind games, the only winning move is not to play.

Chapter 7:

Deception: More than Just Lies

"To see what is in front of one's nose needs a constant struggle."

— George Orwell

When George Orwell wrote his seminal book *1984*, one of his deepest fears was that a totalitarian government might be able to rewrite history by literally destroying every shred of the past and replacing the old news stories with "updated" copies. While this sort of assault on the truth is still possible, and probably more likely than we'd like to admit, history has shown us that deception can come in many forms.

Today the major concern is fake news. Every day we hear about potentially malicious individuals and groups flooding the public discourse with purposefully misleading stories. Instead of seeking out and destroying the truth, modern manipulators flood the airwaves so that the truth gets lost in the shuffle.

We were so busy looking for one form of deception that we missed an entirely new way to spread falsehoods. No matter what your views may be, it's clear that in this day and age we need to maintain constant vigilance against those that would lead us astray.

What Is Deception?

Most people tend to think that deceiving someone is the same as lying to them. The truth is that there is a subtle distinction. Lying to someone means telling them something that isn't true, while deceiving them refers to any approach designed to lead the target to a false understanding of the truth.

When the average person is afraid of the truth they will tell a lie. The danger with lies is that they are relatively easy to call out. As long as it can be proven that reality doesn't match up with the lie, it falls apart. This is why master manipulators use a wide range of tools to deceive. They use more subtle and nefarious ways to clock inconvenient truths and misdirect people away from the reality they're after.

Defining Dark Deception

You might be wondering whether or not deception counts as dark psychology. The word deception definitely sounds dark enough. But you should never be too quick to slap such a heavy label on such a broad category of actions.

For one thing, society requires a certain level of deception. If everyone was completely honest at all times, then we'd likely descend into a violent civil war in a matter of no time. When you tell a sickly individual that they're looking good, you might be saying something deceptive on one level, but if you aren't trying to butter them up to extract some resource from them then you aren't practicing dark deception.

Dark psychology is all about manipulating people in order to get them to do what you want them to do. This means that lies that are told without any intent of changing or controlling anyone's behavior probably doesn't fall under the category of dark psychology.

Common Techniques

Deception comes in many shapes and forms. While you should always be on the lookout for obvious lies, the fact is that the most dangerous forms of deception are much more subtle. The deceiver will use facts, half-truths, and misdirection to keep you from seeing what they are really doing.

With that in mind, let's look at some of the most common deception techniques that you should look out for.

Lies of Omission

It is possible to give someone false ideas without actually making any false statements. This can be done through lies of omission, where the problem isn't what you say but rather what you don't say.

Imagine a man is cheating on his wife with another man. The wife confronts him and asks him "Are you cheating on me?"

The man replies, "Baby, you're the only woman in my life. I promise."

Has the man lied?

He would argue that he has told the truth. He isn't cheating on his wife with another woman. But he didn't actually answer the question that was asked. With linguistic sleight of hand, he subtly changed the subject so that he could give her the wrong idea without technically telling the truth.

This is why you must always pay attention to wording when discussing important matters. The entire legal system has been built up on these sort of language games, with subtle terminology differences drawing the line between freedom and imprisonment.

If you suspect you are being manipulated, then you should always press your accusations, forcing the potential manipulator to clarify their statements until they actually address the heart of the matter. Don't let them skirt the issue, change the subject, or use any sort of language game to try and wiggle their way out. You need to be like a hunting dog when it comes to the truth—absolutely relentless in your search.

Big Lies

In Adolf Hitler's book *Mein Kampf*, he coined the term "große Lüge," or big lie. The idea was that instead of using the typical approach of trying to use small and subtle lies to shift the conversation, a propagandist could control dialogue with one big lie that was so large and brazen that many people would find it hard to believe that someone would attempt such a lie. This concept is based on the idea that people are so used to dealing with the normal lies that they are unprepared for large and abnormal ones (Tinline, 2018).

This tool is especially powerful when used by people in a position of power. When people are faced with a lie from someone they rely upon for a paycheck, they can find it difficult to press back against the lie. It also works well when there is some question of ambiguity, where the lie sounds ridiculous but is difficult to refute with complete certainty.

The other key for this technique is complete confidence. The person making the big lie needs to act like they have unfaltering belief in the statement they are making. Any sign of weakness will allow doubt to creep in, while a steadfast commitment will chip away at the resolve of any individual who has to deal with the lie on a regular basis.

It's also important to remember that a big lie can succeed in deceiving you even if you never totally buy into it. The big lie can achieve huge results simply by shifting the conversation. Think of debate in terms of haggling. A big lie is like demanding a one million dollar paycheck. The person making the demand doesn't need to get the full amount to win, they simply need to get more than they would have gotten if they had asked for a lower amount. As long as the lie moves the conversation in a direction that helps the liar, then they have succeeded.

You may not be dealing with any fascist dictators in your daily life, but that doesn't mean you won't have to deal with big lies. That's why it's important to be skeptical on every level. If you become too fixated on the sort of lies you'd expect to hear on a daily basis, then you may find yourself allowing a big lie to slide. You also need to understand that at some point you need to draw a line. Some people can't be compromised with, as they will only use your willingness to compromise to exploit you.

Mixing Truth and Lies

Just as an assassin will mix poison with wine to make it harder to detect, a manipulator will mix lies with truths to make it more difficult for you to tell which is which.

This is a technique that is commonly used to sell snake oil. Concoctions will be created by mixing together ingredients that are healthy on their own, point out the proven health benefits of the ingredients, and then go on to make dramatic claims about the diseases that their elixir can cure. If the product is new on the market, people will be able to research the claims and find out that most of the claims made can be backed up by science, while the more extreme propositions are neither confirmed nor denied. A lot of people will take this as a reason to trust the seller and invest in their product, not realizing that they have been tricked.

You need a keen ear and a skeptical mind to recognize the most important statements being made. Just because a speech is filled with 100 statements and 99 of them can be proven to be true, it doesn't mean that it's a good and trustworthy speech. If the one controversial statement is the core of the argument being made, then everything falls apart.

Be careful about how facts might be used to lead you into fiction. Manipulators often use chain logic, with one statement leading to another. Follow these chains all the way to the end and make sure that they end in something that's demonstrably true or firmly supported by the previous arguments. Don't allow yourself to get so swept up by a flurry of facts that you allow falsehoods to sneak in.

Small-Scale Deception

As with many things in life, deception isn't black and white. It isn't something that can be quickly and cleanly categorized. Instead, it's better to understand the different types of deception based on things like scale. Some deceptions are clearly small scale, some are definitely large scale, while many fall in between.

You might think that the best approach to take would be focusing on the large scale deceptions and ignoring the small change. But you need to understand that small changes can add up quickly, especially when in the hands of a masterful manipulator. Small-scale deceptions can be some of the most dangerous to deal with because of their apparent unimportance. People are more likely to let such deceptions slide and unwittingly open themselves up to greater threats than they might have imagined.

A Hypothetical

Imagine you are tasked with breaking through a wall. You are allowed to attempt this feat with one of two tools, a sledgehammer or a metal spoon. Which do you choose?

Just about everyone is going to pick a sledgehammer. After all, the job can be finished with a few swings of such a mighty tool. But the more perceptive individual will ask for more context. How can you decide the right tool for busting down a wall if you don't know where the wall is and why you need to tear through it?

Now imagine that you're in a prison cell. The guards are watching you carefully around the clock, granting you only a few moments of anything close to privacy a day. You're tired of being in prison and ready to bust out. But what tool do you use to get through the wall of your prison?

Here we see that a little bit of context changes everything. Suddenly the tool that seemed perfect for the job only moments ago now seems like it will do more harm than good. A sledgehammer might get the job done in a few swings, but those swings are sure to alert the guards and derail the entire escape operation before you've even gotten out of your room.

Suddenly the spoon that seemed comically useless looks like it might be the right tool for the job.

This is the sort of approach that manipulators take when choosing their methods for approaching any given situation. Sometimes they might need to pull out their metaphorical hammer and tell some big lies, but there are many scenarios where carefully applied small scale deceptions can do a lot more damage than a single big falsehood.

It's common for manipulators to use a gradually building approach to deception. They will start with small lies that will start to confuse their target and cloud their vision. It helps if the deceptive statements are so close to the truth or impossible to fact check that the target begins to find it difficult to tell fact from fiction.

A skilled manipulator will slowly break down their target's defenses, hitting them with larger and larger lies until they have them right where the want them. The goal is that eventually they can say just about anything and still be believed, but they understand that they can't jump from step one directly to step 100.

Once again, this brings us back to the importance of constant vigilance and a low tolerance for anything that even smells like manipulation. If you tolerate small scale deceptions then you are just opening yourself up for dealing with bigger and bigger lies. You may also find that while you can handle one or two lies, once you're dealing with a flood of dozens or even hundreds of deceptions, it can be almost impossible to maintain a clear and healthy mindset. And as soon as a manipulator senses that they've weakened you, they will pounce.

Chapter 8:
Brainwashing:
Hollywood Got It Wrong

"[T]he horror of Communism, Stalinism, is not that bad people do bad things — they always do. It's that good people do horrible things thinking they are doing something great." - Slavoj Žižek

Brainwashing. This single word is one of the most frightening in the English language to anyone who has taken the time to think through the implications. Imagine someone taking your brain and wiping it clean of your essential beliefs and personality. Now imagine them rewriting your thoughts to conform to their expectations and desires.

The very concept strikes many as a fate similar to death, with all the things that make you yourself getting replaced. But as you no doubt know, many of the common beliefs surrounding brainwashing don't actually come from reality. If you want to understand real brainwashing, how it works, and how to protect yourself, you need to start by separating fact from fiction.

What REAL Brainwashing Looks Like

Just as cult members need to be carefully deprogrammed so that they can escape the false beliefs planted in their mind by their cult leader, if you want to fully understand dark psychology you need to carefully remove the false beliefs implanted in your mind by Hollywood.

The image of brainwashing that you probably have in your head is incorrect in many ways, and until you have removed the fiction-based beliefs and replaced them with reality-based beliefs you'll never truly understand the process and how you can defend against it.

Fiction: Brainwashing is a Quick Process

In many Hollywood stories, brainwashing happens in a matter of moments. The individual is tied down to a chair and forced to undergo some sort of procedure that reaches into their mind, cleans it out, and turns them into an entirely new person.

Fact: Brainwashing is a gradual process

The reality is that the human mind is a complex thing that no piece of machinery can accurately reprogram. That day might come at some point, but for now brainwashing must be done slowly, methodically, and gradually. If a manipulator tries to speed through the steps, then the procedure might not take or the target's brain could be severely damaged. It's not uncommon for brainwashing to go on for months or even years at a time.

Fiction: Brainwashing only happens to dull or weak minded individuals

When Hollywood isn't pushing the idea that brainwashing can be achieved instantly via pill or laser beam, they may suggest that individuals who succumb to brainwashing do so because of some sort of deficiency. They might be unintelligent, weak willed, or both. This is often done to create contrast between the hero who is able to withstand a brainwashing attempt and the poor unfortunate souls who succumb to it.

Fact: Brainwashing Can Happen to Anyone

A close examination of history reveals that people of all sorts, from all walks of life, have ended up succumbing to brain washing. Looking at many modern cults, you will see that they actually attract some very smart individuals. Doctors, scientists, and computer experts are the sort of people who you might assume would be too naturally skeptical to fall into this sort of trap, but many of these educated individuals actually seek out people who will answer the questions that science can't answer. This honest and well-intentioned quest can lead them into the clutches of dark manipulators. It really can happen to anyone.

Fiction: Brainwashing Can Reprogram Your Mind Against Your Will

To depict the horror of brainwashing, many hollywood stories will show individuals kicking and screaming while it is going on. They do their best to fight against the procedure, but in the end it overwhelms them and wipes their personality away in spite of all the fight that they were able to muster.

Fact: Brainwashing Works Best When It Works With Your WIll

While there are definitely plenty of cases of hostile governments working to brainwash spies using pain and pain alone to convince them to come around, the most successful brainwashing efforts tend to employ a more nuanced approach. Manipulators will try and find out what the person they are trying to control wants and then use this information to create a stick and carrot program of control. In cults, the idea is usually that the target is isolated and then tempted with the idea of belonging. As the mind becomes desperate for companionship, it will start to become more malleable. And once the target is allowed to enjoy the companionship they've worked for, their new peers will pressure them into conforming with the group. It's a setup where the house always wins.

How Brainwashing Actually Works

In real life, brainwashing is a slow and methodical process of breaking down a person's identity and replacing it with something new. It is absolutely essential that you understand that this is a multi-step process. Hollywood gets things completely wrong when they only present one side of the equation, showing people having their identities getting taken from them or having their minds filled with propaganda. The reality is that both of these steps are required for a complete brainwashing process.

One of the first steps of the brainwashing process is isolation. The target needs to be separated from their social structure. After all, friends and family members are going to fight against the process, so the target needs to get away from them. This break can be made all at once, or it can be done gradually. In many cases the manipulator will encourage the target to become more and more hostile with their friends and family, putting up barriers and lashing out so that they themselves are the ones who end up separating themselves from the very people who might be able to save them from what is coming.

Once some degree of isolation has been achieved the manipulator can begin to attack the target's existing identity. The goal is to completely hollow them out so that they can be filled up with whatever the manipulator has in mind later on. Some manipulators will start with an all-out blitz on their identity, while others will slowly build up criticism until every facet of the target's personality has been torn down. Any piece of identity that doesn't fit in with the ideology or plan that the brainwasher has in mind represents a potential threat to the success of their plan, and that's why it must be eliminated. Any identity outside of the group will make it easier to leave the group when the pressure is on, and that's the last thing a dark manipulator wants.

Eventually, the process will move from external criticism to internalized criticisms. The manipulators will try and get the target to confess to their crimes and guilt, telling the whole world that their life is a lie and that they are hollow inside. The idea is that you can only shape a person's thought process so much by telling them how to think. If you really want to transform the way they think, you need to get them to actively play a part in the process. The person being manipulated may have to repeat a mantra or find faults inside of themselves, anything that gets them actively criticizing their old identity so that a split can occur and a new identity can be built.

Deprivation is another important part of the brainwashing process. This means that the target is denied any luxuries and many basic necessities. The brainwashing process often includes starvation and sleep deprivation. The weaker the individual is physically, the lower their mental defenses will be. The body understands the rules to the game on a subconscious level. It knows that if you want to get the food, water, and sleep that you need then you must play along with the people in charge. This leads to the truly frightening situation where the target feels their very body turning against them, encouraging them to give up on their identity so that they can live to see another day.

As the situation becomes more and more difficult, a paradigm shift can take place within the manipulated individual. Through the process so far they might be going along with what they are asked to do in order to get by, even as they secretly reject what they are forced to say and do. But as they repeat their messages and feel their strength draining away, eventually the lines between truth and falsehood begin to blur. Suddenly the words that are coming out of the target's mouth seem less like a lie and more like the truth. With every act of confession and self criticism, the individual begins to shift over into the world that they've only been pretending to exist in so far.

The end of the brainwashing process can feel like a moment of religions transcendence. The old world is left behind and a new realm is entered into. Despair and hope commingle as they realize that they are just a short distance away from the world of the living. All they need to do is confirm that they have passed over into the world that their manipulators have prepared for them.

And so the final step is one of both death and rebirth. The old shell is abandoned and a new life is embraced. When the brainwasher is convinced that the switch has been flipped, they can finally embrace their new convert and welcome them back into the world of the living. Suddenly the target is overwhelmed by all of the positive things that they have been denied for so long. Friendship, affection, food, water, open space, blue skies, it all seems like new and the newly brainwashed individual knows who to thank for everything. All goodness clearly flows from the person who forced them through the brainwashing process. The time spent going through all the pain and suffering might have been no fun, but the overwhelming joy of gaining a new lease on life will make it seem as if all the suffering was worth it.

That's one way that it can happen. While there are many variations that different manipulators may employ, what you have just read is the rough roadmap that is used to brainwash individuals. It is the insidious culmination of countless years of cruel experimentation in mind control. It's an in-depth process that requires a lot of time, energy, and secrecy, but if it can be pulled off the results can be nearly impossible to fully undo.

Manipulators can also tone down the individual steps while maintaining the overall structure of the process. An individual doesn't have to be locked in a room and starved for days in order for the brainwashing process to have an effect. The reality is that the necessary severity of the steps depends on how defensive the individual is. If someone is relatively open to the idea, then they don't need to be pushed to dangerous extremes in order to achieve striking results.

All of this is to say that you should always be on your guard. Even if a situation doesn't seem that serious to you, it may quickly escalate and lead you to a situation that you aren't prepared for. Don't let an open mind lead you to destruction.

Collective Manipulation

A dark persuader can achieve dramatic things by working to manipulate a single individual, but their impact can become supercharged when group dynamics become involved. Every additional person added into the equation might increase the risk that the manipulator will be called out, but it also increases the impact of every manipulative measure that is taken.

At first the different individuals pose a problem. How can everyone be brought into lock-step without running the risk that they'll get together, compare notes, and discover that something is wrong? Many ill-equipped manipulators find their efforts falling apart as they gather together groups of individuals who have the fortitude and independence necessary to overcome the charms of the group's founder. But with time, luck, or sheer force of will, eventually there comes a point where the power of the group is harnessed to strengthen and develop the group.

Collective manipulation takes the basics of manipulation and pumps it up exponentially. It means that instead of just having one individual who is constantly having to reinforce the beliefs against the threats of the outside world, every member of the community can step in and do their part to build up and reinforce the common belief system. Everyone is following behind the leader, but the leader is no longer acting on their own. Every effort the leader makes ends up echoing through the hierarchy that they have set up. Seeing this sort of thing take place before your very eyes is as awe inspiring as it is frightening. It shows you just what humans are capable of achieving once they set their mind to the task at hand.

It's enough to help you understand how manipulators end up believing their own lies. Manipulators aren't always immune from their own charms. Some manipulators end up falling for their own stories once they start being reflected back by their followers. This can create an intense series of reflection and amplification that can lead to some mind boggling places.

Still, despite the seemingly unending power that seems to flow out of the truly committed human mind, eventually reality sets in. Once a group of committed believers ends up dashed against the rocks of reality, the aftermath can be unbelievably messy. Many people never fully recover after being brainwashed. They will spend their whole lives trying to regain some of the normality that they lost when they first gave in to the collective madness.

Once again, you must remember that the individuals who fall prey to brainwashing are not dumb or weak-willed. Some of the smartest and strongest human beings have found themselves allowing their brains to be reprogrammed because they allowed themselves to be swept away by a torrent of emotion and peer pressure that they were unprepared for.

Group mind control is can be like flash flooding. The situation can seem completely manageable one moment, and then the next thing you know a surge of energy comes along that sweeps you away. This is why you should do everything you can to avoid cults and any other groups where a dark manipulator might have their voice amplified by an army of followers.

The Consequences

It's important to remember that manipulation has a cost. The toll that brainwashing can take on a human mind is almost unimaginable. Families can be destroyed, individuals can be hollowed out, and the very bonds of society can dissolve thanks to the efforts of a single dark manipulator.

One of the clearest areas you can see this in is the world of cult-deprogramming. Cult leaders are some of the most infamous manipulators in existence, and if you've ever had the chance to deal with someone who has been in a cult it's easy to see why. Even after someone has physically left the cult there are still emotional connections that exist and are almost impossible to erase. Countless psychological professionals have devoted their careers to helping to ease such individuals back into regular society, and even though they are equipped with all the latest tools in modern mental health they still find it almost impossible to counteract the damage inflicted by a manipulator.

One story that perfectly illustrates the long-lasting impact of brainwashing is that of the remaining members of the Heaven's Gate Cult. It was a UFO religion lead by a man named Marshall Applewhite. The man was a very strange individual by just about anyone's standards, but he still managed to gather together a flock of devoted followers. He didn't attract a large following, but those that stuck by him were willing to give their all to his religion.

Unfortunately, in 1997, Applewhite asked his followers to give their all. They commited suicide in hopes that the act would allow them to leave Earth behind and rise up into a spaceship that was following behind the Hale-Bopp Comet.

Most people know about the many members of Heaven's Gate who killed themselves, but few know about the surviving members. A few individuals weren't told to kill themselves and so they managed to survive the tragedy. You would think that witnessing the mass suicide of their friends would convince them that the man they viewed as a prophet was actually a dangerous madman, but instead of abandoning the group that abandoned them, the survivors decided to double down and recommit themselves to the message of their church.

Over two decades have past since the mass suicide, and there are still two Heaven's Gate members working diligently to preserve the church's website while they wait for the UFO to return and offer them a chance to go and join their friends. They are so committed that they have even been known to sue anyone who infringes on the church's copyrights.

Belief is sturdy. It can stand up to trials that the average person can't comprehend. Brainwashing takes the normal process of belief development and cranks it up to 110%, creating beliefs that are hard to dispel even after they've clearly been proven to be false.

This is the power of brainwashing. This is the danger of brainwashing.

Once a mind has buckled under the full weight of an expertly executed brainwashing, it will never be the same again. Even if the individual can be saved from their toxic beliefs they will be left to carry mental scars for the rest of their life.

Even in situations that aren't as drastic, there are still going to be all sorts of issues that need to be sorted out. Individuals who have been brainwashed usually find out the hard way that their ability to differentiate between what is true and what is false has been clouded by their time undergoing the brainwashing process.

The final thing that's worth remembering is the fact that people who have been mistreated often find it difficult, if not impossible, to trust people again. This is one of the great tragedies brought about by dark psychology. Manipulators prey on the trusting nature of the average human being. They see kindness as a weakness and exploit it for their own personal gain.

Once a person has gone through this process, it becomes difficult to ever trust again, and quite understandably so. Any amount of time spent opening yourself up to a manipulator will teach you to be careful about who you open up to.

Still, it's worth remembering that things can get better. The wounds created by brainwashing may never be completely erased, but they may dull with age. Brainwashing doesn't need to be the end of the road. Instead, it's better to think of your escape from brainwashing as the start of a new life, filled with opportunities for success and joy.

Recovering from brainwashing isn't easy, but with the right people on your side you can retake control of your mind and blaze a path toward a brighter future.

Conclusion:
When Knowledge Becomes Power

"He who fights with monsters should look to it that he himself does not become a monster." — Friedrich Nietzsche

You have now been introduced to the world of dark psychology. By reading through this book, you have initiated yourself into the world of a select few, those who see past the world as the powers that be want you to see and into the dark reality behind the illusion.

If you are like most people who learn these facts, you'll never be able to see the world the same way. Around every corner you'll see manipulators lying in wait. But you don't have to despair. The world may be a dark place, but it's possible to bring some light to it.

What happens from here all depends on how you choose to use your newfound knowledge.

Recognizing Danger and Respecting Power

When looking for reasons why humanity has been able to rise so far above the other living creatures that walk this Earth, many people point to the fact that we were able to harness the power of fire. Most lifeforms that live on this Earth are forced to spend each and every night in pitch darkness, unable to see the world around them. The only animals that were able to be active at night were those that evolved specialized eyes that could see in low-light situations, and these natural mutations often came with drawbacks in other areas.

Everything changed when mankind harnessed the power of fire.

Suddenly the darkness wasn't some invincible force that we had to live with. We didn't have to wait around for the sun to rise up in the morning. We could create our own miniature suns that we could carry with us. A whole new world of possibilities opened up to us.

But while the harnessing of fire eliminated many old dangers, it also created new ones. Fire used to be something humans fled from, but now they were creating fires in their own homes. Instead of seeing flames as a force of nature to be feared, it became easy to see them as a problem that had been solved. The wolf had been turned into a harmless puppy overnight.

At least, that's how it might have seemed to some. The truth is that flames cannot be fully tamed. You can put them to use creating heat, cooking food, and providing light, but if you touch the flames you will be burnt.

The moment you lose your respect for the fire is the moment when you are in grave danger. The same goes for dark psychology.

You must never lose sight of how destructive manipulation can be. Even people with good intentions can end up causing horrific disasters once their manipulative efforts spread beyond their control. Lies can be like flames, you might think you can control them but they can take on a life of their own in an instant.

Manipulating someone is simple when compared to counteracting the effects of manipulation. You may find that if you lie to someone and then try and confess your sins they'll be more likely to believe the original lies than the eventual confession.

Knowledge is power, but power is difficult to harness.

The naturally inclined manipulators of this world make it look easy, but this is usually because their Dark Triad traits help them to ignore the ramifications of their actions. They're like pyromaniacs who start fires without any concern for the long term consequences of their actions. And like pyromaniacs, many pathological manipulators end up burning themselves or facing serious repercussions for their actions.

The truly successful manipulators are the ones who understand restraint and strategy. These are the manipulators you should learn from if you want to take control of your own life, and they are also the ones that you need to look out for if you wish to protect yourself.

Moving Forward

We are coming to the end of this book. You have now been introduced to the most basic concepts of dark manipulation. You can look at the world around you and recognize the coercive intentions behind some of the most innocent actions and events. The feeling of seeing the world for what it truly is can be exhilarating. It can almost feel like a superpower has been given to you, and now you're ready to run out and start leaping over tall buildings in a single bound.

You have just received your basic education in dark manipulation. Meanwhile, the persuaders are out there who have been practicing their craft for years or even decades. If you've just finished your first college class, they have finished their doctorates.

Sometimes knowing a little bit is more dangerous than knowing nothing at all.

If you truly want to understand manipulation, then you must make its study an integral part of your life. This doesn't mean that you have to read psychology textbooks every day until you pass away, it simply means that you need to observe the world around you and the interactions that go on within it through the lens of manipulation.

With every day and each new observation, you will gain a deeper understanding of how the human mind works and how it can be manipulated. The theoretical knowledge you've gained from this book will start to map onto the practical knowledge you gain from real life experience. When that happens, you can really achieve some amazing things.

Out of Darkness

This book was written to shine light on a world of darkness, but you must remember that the first glimpse of light in a dark cave will blind those who are looking on. It takes time for the human eye to adjust to new light and it takes time for the human mind to adjust to new information.

The good news is that by reading this book, you've already taken your first step into a world of greater understanding. Most people in this world never go this far. You don't need to be the world's foremost expert in manipulation to get ahead in this life, you just need to know more than the average person.

In the land of the blind the man with one eye is king. Now that your eye has finally started to blink open, what will you do?

References

Blundell, A. (2015, January 8). What is Machiavellianism in Psychology? Retrieved from https://www.harleytherapy.co.uk/counselling/Machiavellianism-psychology.htm

Everything You Wanted to Know About the Science of Psychopaths. (2018, June 30). Retrieved from https://www.scienceofpeople.com/psychopath/

Hypnosis. (2018, November 01). Retrieved from https://www.mayoclinic.org/tests-procedures/hypnosis/about/pac-20394405

Kelley, R., & Kelley, B. (2018). Just Wrestle: How We Evolved Through Rough And Tumble Play. *Journal of Evolution and Health, 2*(3). doi:10.15310/2334-3591.1073

Narcissistic personality disorder. (2017, November 18). Retrieved from https://www.mayoclinic.org/diseases-conditions/narcissistic-personality-disorder/symptoms-causes/syc-20366662

Rhodewalt, F. (n.d.). Narcissism. Retrieved from https://www.britannica.com/science/narcissism

Sarkis, S. A. (2017, January 22). 11 Warning Signs of Gaslighting. Retrieved from https://www.psychologytoday.com/us/blog/here-there-and-everywhere/201701/11-warning-signs-gaslighting

Tinline, P. (2018, March 17). The art of the big lie: The history of fake news. Retrieved from https://www.newstatesman.com/world/2018/03/art-big-lie-history-fake-news

Vorenberg, M. (2004). Final freedom: The Civil War, the abolition of slavery, and the Thirteenth Amendment. Cambridge: Cambridge University Press.

Yong, E. (2018, December 07). Psychology's Replication Crisis Is Running Out of Excuses. Retrieved from https://www.theatlantic.com/science/archive/2018/11/psychologys-replication-crisis-real/576223/

www.ingramcontent.com/pod-product-compliance
Lightning Source LLC
Chambersburg PA
CBHW031131020426
42333CB00012B/322